More STRIP-PIECED Watercolor Magic

Deanna Spingola

New Designs and Techniques for 30 Watercolor Quilts

That Patchwork Place®

DEDICATION

To our children and growing
number of grandchildren.

ACKNOWLEDGMENTS

Wonderful quilting friends and fellow guild members have contributed to this book by making many of the quilts featured. Some of them suffered personal loss during the time they were also working on the quilts. My affection and profound gratitude go to the following for their hard work and marvelous talents: Nancy Bolliger, Barbara J. Boyd, Pam Bryan, Margaret Couch, Glenda Davis, Carol Deal, Linda K. Garzynski, Denise Griffin, Wanda S. Hanson, Susan L. Harmon, Doris E. Havens, Trisha Horner, Rae A. Kittleson, Dorothy Larsen, Marilyn A. Leccese, Karen Y. Palese, Dee Pitthan, Carol Sherwood, Tracey L. Steinbach, Mary Swanson, Donna Tait, Lorry Taylor, and Barbara Wessel.

Thanks to my wonderful husband, Bob, my best friend, whose vision of a larger sewing space has added immeasurably to my sewing and creating comfort. And to Frank Zafir, a wonderful and creative son-in-law and carpenter, who spent time remodeling two smaller rooms into a wonderful design studio, a special place to work and dream in.

My thanks to That Patchwork Place. Their capable staff simplifies the things that, true to my nature, I usually make more difficult. Sure, that is their job, but they do it in such a pleasant, professional, yet friendly manner. They edit out all the unnecessary (but not uninteresting) opinions, "meaning of life" philosophies, and really irrelevant trivia that would make a very long monotonous, tedious, incessant, mundane, non–quilt related … I am grateful to this wonderful publishing family, who had confidence in my ideas and abilities and gave me a platform to share them with fellow quilters.

Thanks to the following companies who provided some of the beautiful fabric shown in this book: Hoffman Fabrics, Concord Fabrics, P & B Textiles, and Peter Pan Fabrics. Thanks to Lee Anne's Batiks, San Diego, California, for the batik panel.

CREDITS

Editor-in-Chief .... Kerry I. Hoffman
Technical Editor .... Sally Schneider
Managing Editor .... Judy Petry
Design Director .... Cheryl Stevenson
Copy Editor .... Liz McGehee
Proofreader .... Melissa Riesland
Illustrator .... Laurel Strand
Photographer .... Brent Kane
Cover & Text Designer .... Kay Green
Production Assistant .... Marijane E. Figg

MISSION STATEMENT

We are dedicated to providing quality products and service by working together to inspire creativity and to enrich the lives we touch.

More Strip-Pieced Watercolor Magic
©1997 by Deanna Spingola

That Patchwork Place, Inc.
PO Box 118
Bothell, WA 98041-0118 USA

Printed in Hong Kong
01 00 99 98 97   6 5 4 3 2

Library of Congress Cataloging-in-Publication Data
Spingola, Deanna,
      More strip-pieced watercolor magic / by Deanna Spingola.
      p. cm.
      ISBN 1-56477-181-4
      1. Strip quilting—Patterns. 2. Patchwork—Patterns.
3. Color in textile crafts. I. Title.
TT835.S653 1997
746.46'041—dc21   96-37091
                                                                      CIP

TABLE OF CONTENTS

PREFACE

Almost everyone knows a quilter—it may be your mother, sister, aunt, cousin, or spouse—and there seems to be a quilt, or the memory of one, in many of our lives. It may be the one we awakened beneath each morning, or possibly a cherished family heirloom.

We have experienced an unprecedented growth in the great American tradition of quiltmaking. Attendance at classes and quilt shows spans a wide demographic range, with every age group and economic level well represented. Often, picture-taking spouses are as enthusiastic as their companions.

Traditional fabric-shop owners lament that no one seems to be sewing anymore; affordable ready-to-wear imports have attracted former sewing customers. But that doesn't mean we no longer make time to be creative with fabric. Advanced sewing-machine technology, labor-saving tools, and great fabric continue to promote creativity, even in our fast-paced society.

Many of us sewed to save money, solve fitting problems, or to own that special-occasion or designer dress. We also sewed as a creative release, and we continue to sew. But now we create wonderful one-of-a-kind garments; we also cut up fabric and sew it back together into quilts. Yesterday's stitcher has undergone a metamorphosis and has emerged as today's quilter.

We create the so-called traditional quilts that are more likely found on a bed, and the art or contemporary quilts that we display on a wall. Strip-pieced watercolor quilts function beautifully in both areas. The easier strip-piecing method allows us to quickly produce larger bed-size quilts as well as smaller wall-size ones.

Watercolor quilts are people pleasers. They are visually appealing to nearly everyone. However, not every quilter is willing to cut and piece all the individual squares required for a conventional watercolor quilt. In an effort to create watercolor quilts without cutting individual squares, I developed a strip-piecing method.

My first book, *Strip-Pieced Watercolor Magic*, was merely the beginning of a marvelous, exciting adventure that I continue to enjoy. The tremendous response to the first book inspired this second one, which contains new patterns and techniques. These new designs provide more options for the beginner as well as for the advanced quilter. Some of the quilts appear more complicated, yet they are all relatively easy to create. Anyone who can rotary cut accurately, follow diagrams, and sew carefully can create a strip-pieced watercolor quilt.

STRIP-PIECED WATERCOLOR MAGIC

We are all in the process of becoming wonderful quiltmakers. No matter when we began that exhilarating journey, with proper preparation, appropriate tools, suitable fabric, and a visionary concept, each of us can create remarkable quilts.

Even if you have quiltmaking experience, review this entire book so you have a good understanding of the fabric-selection principles, strip-piecing techniques, and block-construction concepts. Then evaluate your stash for appropriate fabrics.

The most challenging, yet the most critically important element in creating these quilts is fabric selection. It can be an intimidating task, even for the most experienced quilter. Watercolor quilts require a wide variety of multicolor prints. It is this vast combination of fabrics that produces the beauty of a watercolor quilt.

People often ask how I combine so many fabrics in one quilt. They also accuse me of using rather unusual fabrics. I admit it. There are few absolutes and many options when it comes to fabric selection. There is not an exclusively perfect fabric for a particular position. You can produce a surprisingly attractive quilt despite some peculiar fabric choices.

Aristotle said "To learn to play the flute, you have to play the flute." So it is with anything we wish to learn, including choosing fabric. We must persevere, and yet be patient with ourselves as we acquire this skill. We learn something with every quilt we make.

The need for a variety of fabrics provides the perfect opportunity to utilize the pieces many of us have stashed away, waiting to create just the perfect quilt. Pat Davis, a witty quilting friend, told me we should no longer refer to this stockpile as our stash, but as our resources. I must concede, it does give our gathering tendencies a ring of legitimacy. As a young mother, I used to can fruits and vegetables. Inevitably, when I picked fruit, such as cherries, I picked twice as many as necessary. The fruit on the next branch always looked so inviting. It didn't matter if I eventually had enough cherries for the entire city of Boise. Fabric has the same effect on me. Am I the only obsessed fabric collector? I doubt it. I know there are many of you out there; I meet you every day.

Use this book as a resource for your own creativity. Most strip-pieced watercolor quilts are geometric rather than pictorial. However, some designs are more pictorial, such as "Wandering Through the Fence" (page 74). Feel free to combine geometric and pictorial watercolor techniques. Create a pictorial design with 2" squares and enclose it in strip-pieced blocks. Change the designs if you choose. If you are not a fan of square quilts, add an extra row at the top and bottom to make it rectangular. If you like the center four blocks of a particular quilt and would like to create a small wall hanging, use just those blocks. You can also make a smaller quilt by cutting narrower strips.

EQUIPMENT

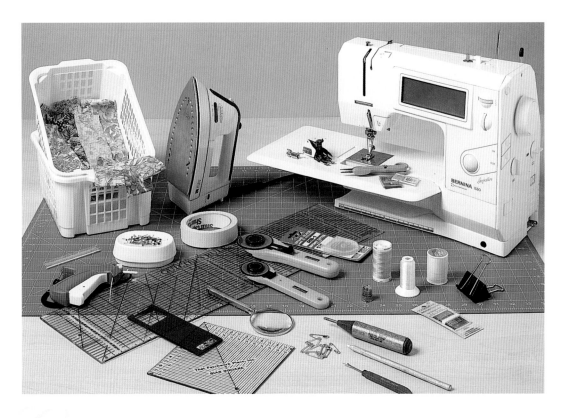

Every artist needs appropriate supplies. Equipment for strip-pieced watercolor quilts includes the following:

Rotary Cutter: This is the timesaving tool we all wish we had invented. I prefer the larger model with a 2¼"-diameter blade. Keep an extra blade on hand and change it regularly. Sharp blades are a necessity, especially for cutting multiple layers. If the blade does not move easily through the fabric or if it skips or produces ragged edges, change it.

Cutting Mat: Use a self-healing, 24" x 36" cutting mat. This size accommodates 44"-wide fabric, as well as the finished groups of strip sets. A mini-mat will not accommodate multilayer cutting or the stacked strip sets.

Rulers—6" x 24" and 6" Square: I prefer the Quilter's Rule products for measuring, because the ridges on the bottom keep the ruler from slipping around. Use the same ruler throughout the cutting process, since there may be slight variations between different products.

Sewing Machine: Use a dependable and efficient sewing machine and know how to operate and maintain it. For consistency and accuracy, use the same machine throughout the entire project.

Fabric: Choose high-quality, 100% cotton fabrics. Cotton is available in a wide variety of colors and print styles and produces the best results. See "Fabric Characteristics" on page 8 for more information.

Thread: Use good-quality, 100% mercerized cotton thread for piecing and quilting. I prefer tan or beige for piecing light fabrics, and smoky grays for dark fabrics. Although you might be tempted to use bargain thread, it can be abrasive, lacks uniformity, and is hard on a sewing machine and ultimately on your fabric. Save money somewhere else. For free-motion machine appliqué, use some of the gorgeous specialty threads available. For machine quilting, use an appropriate-weight thread in whatever style appeals to you.

Invisible nylon or polyester thread, size .004 in clear or smoke color, is an excellent choice for machine quilting any multi-fabric quilt. This fine, flexible thread blends beautifully with the many values and colors used in a watercolor quilt. I often use it in the top spool, with a fine cotton embroidery thread in the bobbin. I have also used it successfully both on the top and in the bobbin. Some machines easily handle this thread in the bobbin, and some don't.

If you hand quilt, use 100% cotton quilting thread in whatever color strikes your fancy.

Hand-Quilting Needles: While these needles are available in sizes 3–12, quilters most commonly use sizes 8–10. The larger numbers indicate shorter needles, and the shorter the needle, the shorter the stitch. Choose an appropriate size according to your experience and skill level.

Machine Needles: Size 70/10 or 80/12 are best for both piecing and machine quilting. Change the needle as you begin each new project, after approximately six hours of continuous sewing, or when you hear the needle pop or thud into the fabric. Needle size and thread type should be compatible. Use a larger-eyed needle for specialty threads, such as metallics.

Steam Iron and Ironing Board: Use a good, clean steam iron and sturdy board with a clean cover. Steam not only produces better results, but also preshrinks the fabrics. Press by lifting the iron, then setting it down in another location. Do not slide the iron from one area to another.

Safety Pins: Use 1½" pins to secure the crosscut strips before sewing the actual quilt blocks. Smaller 1" pins mark the top left square of each finished block. Use 1" or 1½" pins to pin-baste the quilt sandwich together.

Kwik Klip™: Use this handy tool to fasten and unfasten safety pins. It prevents sore fingers caused by manipulating a multitude of pins.

Quiltak™: This is my favorite time- and energy-saving method of sandwiching the quilt. Whether you prefer to hand or machine quilt, this remarkable tool secures the quilt top, batting, and backing together by inserting a short plastic tab through the three layers. It is faster than basting with safety pins, and the tabs are easier to maneuver around. Remove the tabs after completing the project. This tool is well worth the investment.

Quiltak Basting Grid: A basting grid lifts the quilt off the work surface, allowing the needle to go through all three layers. The small (7¼" x 22")

Quiltak grids are convenient for small quilts. For larger quilts, buy a 24" x 48" ceiling grid from the hardware store. The one I use is silver and measures ¾" x ¾" x ½" deep. Attach long pieces of cord to each side of the grid to move it around under the quilt sandwich.

Seam Ripper: Every stitcher has experience with this tool. I recently purchased one with a battery-operated miniflashlight in it. What will they think of next?

Thimble: Select one that fits comfortably on the middle finger of your sewing hand.

Small Scissors or Thread Clippers: These are much handier at the machine than large scissors, and they save the blades of your good scissors from nicks caused by repeated thread clipping.

Ruby Beholder®: The Ruby Beholder is a versatile tool for determining the value range of fabric. Hold it close to your eyes to look at the fabric. However, remember that it makes fabrics in the red family look very light, and greens look very dark. Use the 1½" window at the opposite end when considering the motif spacing and appropriateness of a selected print.

Photocopy Machine: Make photocopies of your fabrics to develop your eye for value and motif style. Despite their limitations, both the Ruby Beholder and the photocopy machine are useful in this task.

Design Wall: Get a better perspective of your developing design by placing the pieces on a design wall. Use it to preview or to rearrange completed blocks for optional quilt layouts. Use Thermolam® Plus, felt, or Pellon® secured to foam core, rigid cardboard, or a wall. I use 72"-wide felt secured to a 198"-long wall.

Reducing Glass: Most art pieces, including watercolor quilts, develop an entirely different perspective when viewed from a distance. Use a reducing glass to visually increase the distance between you and your work. You can find it at art-supply stores and some quilt shops. Get a similar perspective by facing away from your work and looking back at it through a hand mirror; or look through a camera lens, the wrong end of a pair of binoculars, or a door peephole purchased at the hardware store.

Boxes or Baskets: After cutting the strips, fold and store the sorted fabric in six value-assigned boxes or baskets, with one value in each basket. These function as your palette.

FABRIC CHARACTERISTICS

The success of any quilt begins with fabric selection. Beautiful quilts do not just happen; they are planned. A significant part of that planning is deciding what fabrics to use.

Watercolor quilts require a large variety of colors, values, and motifs; however, because of the quantity required, the importance of each fabric is reduced. A few less-than-wonderful choices become inconsequential when they are combined with so many other fabrics. The designs interact with each other, creating an overall artistic impression.

Color

Colors are separated and identified by their characteristics on the color scales. The four color scales are pure hues, tones, tints, and shades.

Pure hues contain no additives to dilute their strength or saturation. Black, white, and gray are added to pure hues to create tones, tints, and shades. Pure hues are the intense, brilliant colors associated with summer. Birds, butterflies, ripe fruits, luscious garden vegetables, and glorious seasonal flowers offer a magnificent visual display composed of these pure hues.

Pure rainbow hues are very appropriate in a watercolor quilt. Although we do not ordinarily think of bright, pure colors in Impressionistic art, they are dramatic when skillfully used.

Some quilters feel insecure about using bright colors. As it is in nature, bright color is a beautiful accent in a quilt. While an isolated bright color stands out in a quilt, several used together create a wonderful effect. I have a passion for the energetic pure-hue scale, so I use it in my watercolor quilts. "Summer Symphony" (page 58) is a good example of abundant, but blended pure hues.

Tones remind us of winter, when color fades from almost everything but our memory and the fabric store. Tones are pure hues with varying amounts of gray added. The intensity of the color diminishes with the addition of gray. Generous use of toned fabrics give that wonderful misty look found in "Wandering Through the Fence" (page 74).

Toned fabrics are wonderful for watercolor.

Tints are associated with spring. Their softer colors are created by adding varying amounts of white to pure hues; the amount determines the depth of color. The darkest tints, those that are a little lighter than the original pure hue, are created by adding a small amount of white to the pure color. Very pale tints, called blushes, are produced by adding a very small amount of pure hue to white.

Off-white or beige fabrics lack the clarity of tints because they are usually toned yellows. When a true tint is used adjacent to an off-white, the off-white appears dirty. However, because of the large variety of colors and values in a watercolor quilt, this dirty characteristic remains relatively inconspicuous and should not be a great concern.

Off-whites are really tones rather than tints.

Shades are created by adding black to pure hues. Orange becomes rust, red becomes cranberry, and green becomes hunter. Shades imply strength and provide definition, blending, and contrast.

Dark and light tints

Blushes

Shades create structure and imply strength.

The visual temperature of colors affects how they appear to us. Cool colors, such as blue, green, and purple, appear to retreat. "A World of Hope and Dreams" (page 50) is a wonderful example of a cool-temperature quilt. Warm colors, such as yellow, orange, or red, appear to advance. Since warm colors, as well as brights, stand out, an isolated red, yellow, or orange becomes conspicuous. Use two or more together for a dramatic effect.

Value

Like scissors blades that work together, color and value work together to create the watercolor effect. Value is determined by the lightness or darkness of a fabric. A visually light fabric is high value; a visually dark one is low value. Value is significant to the creation of watercolor quilts because the arrangement of the values defines the pattern.

Cool Fabric Run   Warm Fabric Run

Use this fabric run to assist you in assigning values to your fabrics.

Yellow demands our attention, whether it's McDonald's golden arches, a glorious sunset, spring daffodils, or warning signs. I use yellow as an accent in many of my watercolor quilts to warm up the overall surface.

Combine both warm and cool fabrics equally, or use one temperature predominantly. They work well together in nature; they will also be attractive in your quilt. Most of the quilts in this book feature both warm and cool colors.

In this book, I use six value categories. Each quilt pattern has an accompanying "Fabric Value Key" to assist you in selecting appropriate fabrics.

Fabric Value Key

- ◼ Dark Dark
- ▦ Light Dark
- ▨ Dark Medium
- ▦ Light Medium
- ⬚ Dark Light
- ☐ Light Light

Different-value fabrics play various roles in the production of your quilt. Medium-value prints are always the stars; their motif styles are the most visible. Dark and light values are the supporting cast and are less visible from a distance. Their motif styles are not as readily apparent. Because of this, you can get by with less variety in the very light and very dark values.

Value is relative. Depending on the comparative value of its neighbors, a fabric may perform as a dark medium in one section of a quilt, while in another section, it may be a light dark. See how the relative value of the center strips changes in the photos on page 10.

Multicolor prints frequently contain more than one value. Multivalue prints make it easier for the quilter to blend either lighter- or darker-value adjacent fabrics. These multivalue fabrics are called transitional prints.

To assign a value to a multicolored print, focus on the predominant value within that print.

Classify transitional prints by their predominant value.

Avoid using prints that contain very distinct light-light value areas when the pattern calls for a dark-dark value. As the strips are cut and then cross-cut for the quilt block, the finished square may not contain the right value. You would then have a "sore-thumb" square. One or two of these squares in a quilt is not catastrophic, but they can detract from the design. You should also avoid dark-medium motifs printed on very light backgrounds. The light background appears to advance, becoming more prominent than the motif, especially when it is adjacent to more consistent dark-medium prints.

Many prints combine several values.

Avoid high-contrast prints.

Avoid dark-value motifs on a light background.

Contrast

To provide interest and movement, a quilt must have value contrasts. The selected values do not have to be used in equal amounts; a small amount of high value in a predominately low-value quilt is often enough to create an interesting contrast. A small amount of low value in a predominately high-value quilt has the same effect. Spectacular watercolor quilts, by design, contain contrasting values from high to low; it is this characteristic that gives them their remarkable appeal.

All the quilts in this book contain areas of high and low contrast. A gradual blending of values, from high to low, produces an area that is, by all appearances, low contrast in spite of the range of values selected. This subtle blending is seen in "Deck the Halls" (page 42) as the high values gradually blend while moving away from the high-contrast corners of the central square.

Create high contrast by placing opposite values next to each other. Alternating the values creates the illusion of depth. The center fan in "A World of Hope and Dreams" (page 50) is composed of high-contrast areas, while the circular motion in "Centrifugal Colors" (page 68) is created by the intersection of opposing values. That feeling is further accentuated by the quilting lines.

Illusion

Like the magician who makes things seem what they are not, some of the quilts in this book appear to have curved lines, but they are really strategically positioned squares. The scalloplike border of "Sunrise Serenade" (page 34) and the larger circles in "A World of Hope and Dreams" (page 50) are formed by rectangular units.

Texture

When quilters talk of texture, they are speaking of that fabric characteristic created by the combination of color, value, and style lines either woven into or printed on the fabric. Because solids lack this important characteristic, they are not appropriate for a watercolor quilt unless they are used for special effect. Otherwise, they product flat, uninteresting spaces. As a rule, avoid solids or any fabrics that appear solid from a distance, such as monochromatic prints. These fabrics combine a few values from one color family and appear almost solid when viewed from a distance. If you must use them, do so only in the very dark or very light values.

Avoid fabrics that "read" as solids.

Motifs

A motif is the repetitive pattern that is woven into or printed on the fabric. There are a wide variety of motifs available; however, not all of them are appropriate for strip-pieced watercolor quilts.

Some prints have substantial amounts of background fabric showing or have very large motifs with large solid-colored areas. Avoid these fabrics, because the finished square could appear as a solid.

Avoid fabric that shows too much background.

Avoid extra-large motifs.

The combination of several motif sizes and bright colors conveys energy and motion, while toned colors with petite motifs produce more delicate and subtle quilts.

Select small, medium, and large motifs.

There are three main types of motifs: integrating, linear, and self-contained. Integrating motifs incorporate the abundant curved lines naturally found in flowers, leaves, and fruit. Use those that are printed in a random pattern so that two squares cut from the same fabric would not be identical. Their lines interact and mingle, suggesting movement and vitality. Integrating motifs are easier to combine with each other and with other prints. Their flowing lines suggest uninterrupted movement as the prints advance across the surface of the quilt. Quilts composed of predominately transitional prints are visually comfortable.

Fabric containing integrating motifs include:

- *Florals:* Look for florals in pure hues, subtle tones, fresh tints, and velvety shades. Their fluid lines and color variety make them easy to use. Often, the more traditional calicoes (if they are randomly printed and contain at least three colors) can be used in the light values. Combine them with the more contemporary fabrics.

Multicolor florals in several sizes are the most popular fabrics.

Combine traditional light-colored calicoes with contemporary fabrics.

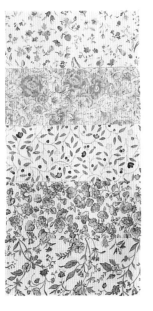

- *Fruits and Vegetables:* The vivid hues, multiple colors, and natural style lines of fruit and vegetable motifs make them a good choice, comparable to florals in their transitional qualities.

Fruit and vegetable fabrics are very colorful, fluid, even luscious.

- *Vines and Leaves:* Vine and leaf prints, providing they contain three or more colors, work well. If the three colors are not definitive, these prints are more acceptable in the darker value, where they imply shade.

Multicolored vines and leaves are good choices.

- ***Theme and Novelty Prints:*** Prints denoting specific holidays or events are usually colorful and fit into the fluid-style motif. Christmas prints often contain more than just the traditional red and green and can work in a watercolor quilt.

Theme prints often employ a variety of great colors.

- ***Creatures:*** Fabrics displaying things that run, crawl, swim, fly, hop, or swing through the trees, as well as stylized animals, are appropriate for watercolor quilts. These include butterflies, bright-hued birds, brilliantly colored fish, exotic jungle prints, and teddy bears.

Animal kingdom prints are useful whether stylized or authentic.

- ***Miscellaneous:*** This group includes paisleys, landscapes, multicolor marbleized prints, swirls, and everything else that doesn't fit into another integrating, fluid category. Sky, rocks, feathers, and water usually have curved, fluid features, but many of this motif type are not multicolored. They fall into the monochromatic category and are not as useful.

These multicolor fluid prints also work well.

Linear motifs, such as plaids and checks, are more structured than the friendly integrating style. Linear prints are composed of straight lines that intersect, creating a pattern. Some are composed of both straight and curved lines and are therefore more pleasing. If you use a majority of linear motifs, your quilt will appear very structured and static. While many quilters appreciate linear prints, they are better used elsewhere.

Linear Prints
Use somewhere else.

Geometric styles, another family of linear motifs, include cubes, triangles, and squares and work better than linear prints. Some abstract geometrics combine curved lines in their design. Batiks and many ethnic prints effectively incorporate geometric designs and contain appropriate choices.

Geometric Prints
These can work in
watercolor quilts.

Self-contained motifs include stripes and small, symmetrical patterns that are generally static. While they may be appropriate for other quilt styles, they are difficult to use in a watercolor quilt.

Self-Contained Motifs
Use somewhere else.

Above all, don't become obsessed with finding the perfect fabric before you begin your quilt. Use what you have stashed and make that quilt. You will learn from it and develop your quiltmaking skills.

YOUR FABRIC COLLECTION

Sorting

Organizing your fabric is an essential task when making watercolor quilts. The process of sorting gives you experience in classifying fabrics. When I first started making watercolor quilts, I sorted my fabric into just six designated values: Dark Dark, Light Dark, Dark Medium, Light Medium, Dark Light, and Light Light. Since I have gained more experience making these kinds of quilts, I now sort by predominant color temperature as well as by value. You don't need to adopt this seemingly compulsive behavior; if you simply sort your fabrics into six value divisions, you can create stunning strip-pieced watercolor quilts.

 PHOTOCOPY EACH GROUP OF fabrics to check your value assignment.

If you have been quilting for a while, you probably have a fabric stash. To sort it, put all your fabric on your work space, such as a table. Eliminate all solids or fabrics that appear as solids from a distance, small symmetrical motifs, very large florals, fabrics with large portions of solid background, and any fabric with less than three colors. Sort the remaining fabric into light, medium, and dark. Then sort each of those groups into light and dark, yielding the six value divisions. If you have nothing left to sort, go shopping! Study the "Fabric Characteristics" section on pages 8–15 and the "Purchasing Fabric" section at right to select appropriate fabrics. Select a favorite quilt from the gallery and shop for the necessary values called for in the materials list.

Purchasing Fabric

I do not shop with a specific project in mind. I purchase what makes my heart beat faster when I need a fabric fix. Because I make a lot of watercolor quilts, I always purchase at least ½ yard. However, since each quilt in the book requires just one 2"-wide strip of each fabric, you may purchase as little as the store will sell you, usually ⅛ yard. You are seeking a variety of prints rather than a large quantity of an individual print.

The most challenging values to locate are light light and dark dark. In spite of the fabrics available, it is still hard to find sophisticated light-light prints.

Although I encourage you to shop for value rather than color, we all have favorite colors and find it hard to change our buying habits. Choose a wider variety of colors and patterns and remember to choose prints with a minimum of three colors.

Preparing Fabric

Like many things in quiltmaking, prewashing fabric is a matter of choice. Many quilters appreciate the stability provided by the manufacturer's sizing; others wash and then spray-starch the fabric to regain the stability lost by washing.

I have enough trouble just getting the regular laundry washed without worrying about clean fabric. Besides, small pieces become tangled in the washer, and the threads create a jungle in the dryer. But if you are up to that kind of challenge, go ahead and prewash.

If you are concerned about colors running, particularly red, blue, and green, then prewash those. To check dye stability, pin a small swatch of the questionable fabric to a piece of white fabric and wash the fabric the way you intend to wash the finished quilt. If the white fabric is no longer white, continue to wash the colored fabric until the water is clear, then dry it in the dryer or press it dry.

STRIP PIECING YOUR WAY TO A WATERCOLOR QUILT

Most of the quilts in this book are constructed with 2"-wide strips cut across the width of 44"-wide fabric (the crosswise grain). Several quilts also require 1½"-wide strips. Check the quilt plans to determine the correct strip width as well as strip length for your particular project.

Accurate, consistent cutting and stitching are essential. Inaccuracies become apparent when you are sewing the blocks together to create the quilt top, and with so many seams, the inconsistencies multiply quickly.

Cutting the Strips

When cutting the strips, work in a well-lit area and take your time. Fold the fabric in half, not in quarters. This helps prevent crooked strips. Line up the selvages and position the fabric on the cutting mat with the fold closest to you. Place the bulk of the fabric to the right of the ruler if you are right-handed, or to the left of the ruler if you are left-handed. Place a line of the 6"-square ruler on the fold, close to the cutting edge. Butt the 6" x 24" ruler against the 6" square. Remove the square and make a clean cut, rolling the rotary cutter away from your body.

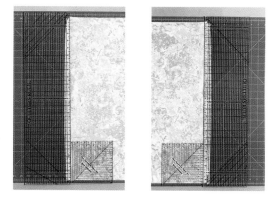

Right-handed cutting   *Left-handed cutting*

As you cut, allow your fingers to walk up the ruler to steady it. The cutting hand

should be opposite the hand holding the ruler. This stabilizes the ruler. Do not lift the cutter from the fabric; hold it in place as your fingers move along the ruler.

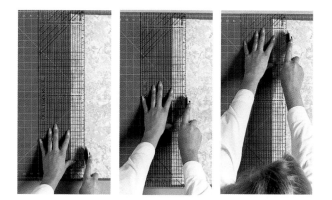

Because cutting single strips is labor-intensive, cut several layers of fabric at a time. I never cut less than six fabrics (twelve layers) at one time. I have cut as many as thirteen fabrics (twenty-six layers). This may sound foolhardy, but the rotary blade can easily handle it.

To cut multiple layers:

- Make sure the blade is very sharp.
- When preparing to cut, position the ruler at least ½" in front of the stacked fabric so you do not inadvertently clip off the corner of the ruler with the rotary blade.
- Stagger the fabric folds ¼" apart when positioning them on the cutting mat.

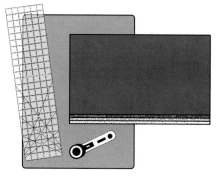

Stagger and cut in multiple layers.

- Keep the folds parallel to prevent crooked strips.

Cut a crooked strip in half and use both parts.

- Place layers of fabric under the opposite edge of the ruler to keep it level. Do not allow the cutter to lean to either side; this can result in inaccurate cuts.

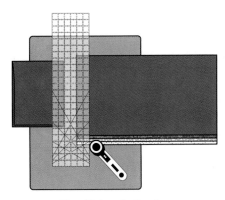

Place fabric under the other
side of the ruler to keep it level.

After cutting the 2"-wide strips, fold them and place them in their designated basket or box. Viewing the strips together is helpful; if one piece stands out from the rest, move it to a more appropriate basket. Use these baskets or boxes as your palettes.

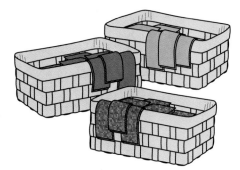

Arranging the Strips

I have used two block types in the quilts in this book: basic strip-pieced multi-fabric blocks and foundation paper-pieced blocks.

Most of the quilts are made from the strip-pieced block, in which the design is created by the strategic placement of values. Rather than cutting numerous small squares, use strips of fabric to construct strip sets. Make one strip set for each row of the block. Stack the strip sets, crosscut them into segments, then assemble them into blocks. Sew the blocks together to complete the quilt.

The following example of the Mediator block shows how to arrange the strips. The block has eight rows across and eight rows down, so you need sixty-four different fabrics to construct the eight strip sets. Although the block requires several strips of each value, each strip is a different print. The numbers across the top of the block diagram indicate the row or strip-set number. The letters "U" for up and "D" for down indicate the pressing direction for that particular strip set.

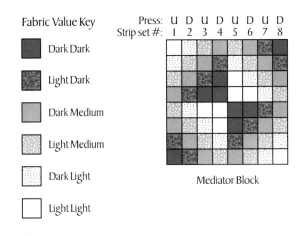

Fabric Value Key

- Dark Dark
- Light Dark
- Dark Medium
- Light Medium
- Dark Light
- Light Light

Press: U D U D U D U D
Strip set #: 1 2 3 4 5 6 7 8

Mediator Block

Referring to the Fabric Value Key, arrange the fabrics for the first strip set. Select a light-light fabric strip and position it on the table. Next, select a dark-light strip and place it on top of the first fabric, staggering it so there is at least 1½" of the first fabric showing. Continue choosing and placing fabrics for the entire row. Lay out the fabrics for the second row next to the first, staggering each fabric as you did for the first row. Lay out the remaining rows. Review the values from top to bottom and from side to side. This is a preview of your completed block. Use the Ruby Beholder to evaluate your choices, and then make any necessary adjustments. Avoid duplicating any of the fabrics within a block.

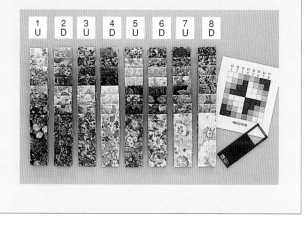

Choose each fabric carefully, but be decisive. Don't be excessively fussy. One particular fabric will neither make nor destroy a quilt. While each fabric contributes to the whole, an individual one becomes insignificant in the context of the entire quilt.

In several quilts, the block rotation results in the same fabric occupying the middle four squares. Choose transitional, randomly printed fabric for this area, especially if the value is light or medium. If you don't like the result after you have completed the blocks, replace those four squares, or sew four 2" squares together and appliqué them over the faulty four. I have even done this after the quilting was completed.

Assembling the Strip Sets

Sewing Guidelines

Establish an accurate ¼" seam guide and mark it on the bed of the sewing machine. Do this even if your machine is equipped with a ¼" foot.

1. Cut a piece of ¼" graph paper 2½" x 5." Place the paper under the presser foot, lower the foot, and insert the needle just to the right of the first line on the right-hand edge of the paper. Make sure the paper is straight and not at an angle.

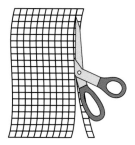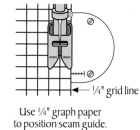

←— ¼" grid line

Use ¼" graph paper to position seam guide.

2. Position a piece of Dr. Scholl's® Molefoam® (available at the drugstore) or layers of masking tape along the right edge of the paper, in front of the feed dogs. If you use masking tape, build a four- to five-layer wall of tape. You may also use a commercial seam guide or Sew Perfect.

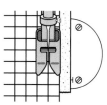

Put masking tape along the edge of the paper to guide fabric. Extend tape behind the needle for 2".

   If the feed dogs do not extend beyond the right edge of the foot, butt the tape right up against the foot and extend it about 1" beyond the back of the foot. This keeps the fabric straight throughout the sewing process. If the feed dogs extend beyond the edge of the presser foot, cut out a section of the tape or Molefoam to fit around them. Do not cover the feed dogs.

   Use the same machine throughout the piecing and assembly process. I try to sew all the strip sets for a quilt at the same time so I do not disturb the position of the Molefoam.

Check the accuracy of your seam allowance. Cut 3 strips, each 2" x 6". Sew them together, using the ¼"-wide seam allowance you have marked or the seam guide of your choice. Press seams to one side, then measure the resulting strip set. It should be exactly 5" wide. If it is not, experiment with different seam-allowance markings. Test again and repeat until your strip set is 5" wide.

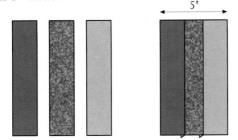

Sewing the Strips Together

Sew the strips for each set together in the order you arranged them. If you do not plan to sew the strip sets immediately, carefully stack each one in order, from top to bottom, put a rubber band around them, and attach the label.

1. Put a small safety pin through the top edge of strip #1 to avoid sewing subsequent strips to the wrong edge. Leave it in, even when you press the strip set, to indicate the top of the set.

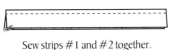

2. Adding strip #2 to the bottom of strip #1, sew the strips together along one long edge.

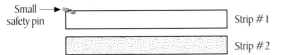

Sew strips #1 and #2 together.

3. Continue sewing strips to the *bottom edge* of the set in the proper order. As you complete each set, pin the label to it, then continue to sew the remaining sets for each quilt. Leave the labels attached until you are ready to cut the segments.

4. Press the finished strip sets from the wrong side to set the stitches, then press from the right side. Make sure there are no pleats. Press the seam allowances of each set in the direction indicated by the U or D on the label. Press all the finished sets at one time. Refer to "Pressing Tips" below.

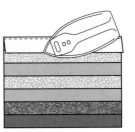 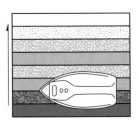

Set the seams on the wrong side of the fabric.   Press the seams to one side from the right side of fabric.

Tip   BOWED SETS ARE USUALLY CAUSED BY incorrect tension on the sewing machine or by using different weights or qualities of fabric. If you have bowed sets, try alternating the stitching direction of every other strip. Or, pin the strips every 2" or 3", removing the pins as you sew. You may also use a walking foot.

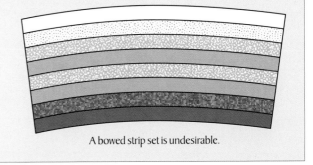

A bowed strip set is undesirable.

Pressing Tips

- Carefully press each strip set in the direction indicated (up or down). To press, set the iron down, lift it, and then set it down in another location. Do not move the iron from side to side; it may distort the fabric.
- Use steam when you press; steam is more effective for flattening seams than dry pressing. Steam pressing will not distort the fabric unless you pull and stretch it as you press.

Constructing the Blocks

1. After completing all the strip sets for the block you are making, place strip set #1 wrong side up on the cutting mat, with the bottom of the set toward you. Position strip set #2 wrong side up on top of strip set #1, but offset about ¼" below it so the seam allowances are not on top of each other creating excess bulk. Continue stacking the strip sets, wrong side up, in numerical order, offsetting each one ¼".

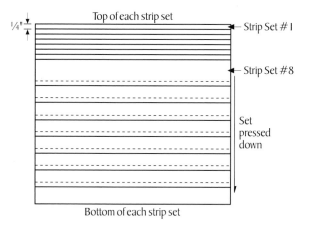

Stagger the strip sets ¼" and position them wrong side up, with the first set on the bottom and the last set on the top.

❧ Note ❧

It is essential that the seam allowances remain parallel for this method of cutting. Take extra care to make sure the seam allowances are parallel for the entire length of the strip sets.

2. Align the rulers as you did to cut strips, and then trim the edges, making a clean cut as described on page 17.

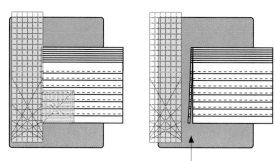

Trim edge.

3. Cut the appropriate-size segments from the strip sets. (Check your pattern.) Most segments are 2" wide, but some are 1½" wide. Cutting multiple layers may be intimidating, but if you remember to position fabric under the opposite edge of the ruler to level it out and if your blade is sharp, there should be no problem.

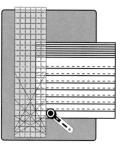

Cut 2"-wide segments.

4. After you cut each segment, pin the layers together with a 1½" safety pin. Insert the pin into the wrong side of the top square of the last set. Push it through to the first set and close the pin. Each closed pin contains all the rows for the entire block in their proper sewing order.

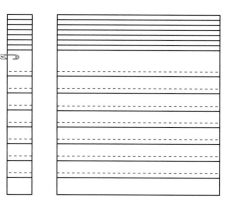

5. Check the edge of the strip set after every three to four cuts to make sure you are still making 90° cuts. Align a horizontal line of the ruler with any internal seam and trim as needed.

6. With the strips right side up, open the safety pin but do not remove it. The first strip off the pin is the first row, the second strip is the second row, and so on to the last row.

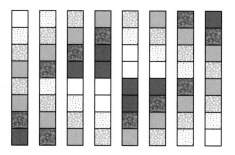

7. Remove the second strip and sew it to the right side of the first strip, matching seam allowances. Pin if necessary. If you followed the pressing plan for each strip set, opposing seams will be pressed in opposite directions.

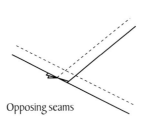

Opposing seams

8. Mark the top square of the first row with a small safety pin to avoid sewing subsequent segments to the wrong edge. Leave this pin in place until you assemble the quilt.

9. Join the remaining segments to complete the block.

If you have distorted blocks, sew alternating rows in opposite directions. Do not press the seam allowances between the rows yet. Wait until you are ready to assemble the quilt top.

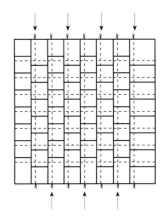

10. Each quilt plan includes dots to identify the top left corner of each block. This corresponds to the safety pin in the top left of each block. When the blocks are completed, arrange them in the order indicated by the marked corners and block number on the quilt plan.

11. Press all vertical seams in each block in one direction; then, wherever possible, press the vertical seams of the adjacent blocks in the opposite direction. Because of the way some blocks rotate within the quilt design, connecting blocks may have seam allowances pressed in the same direction. It is unavoidable in some circumstances. Either live with the bulk or twist the seam allowances to make them nest properly.

You may reposition your layout, wrong side out, to coordinate the pressing directions of all the rows. Remember, the seams in each row and each block interact with the row above and below.

Tip

I SEW FOUR BLOCKS at once, chain piecing the blocks together. Sew the first two rows of each of the four blocks in a long chain, without breaking the threads in between, then sew the third row to each of the blocks. Continue adding consecutive rows until the block is complete, then cut the threads between the blocks.

Chain-piece when possible.

The Quilt Plans

Construct all the blocks for the quilt you are making, following the directions in "Strip Piecing Your Way to a Watercolor Quilt" on pages 17–22. Pay particular attention to the size of the strips required as well as the cutting size of the segments. They are not always all the same, even within the same quilt.

Some design blocks are found in more than one quilt. Plan ahead and save time by making enough blocks for two different quilts that contain the same blocks.

All but two of the quilts require two or more design blocks. You may duplicate the fabric from block to block or use different fabrics for the additional blocks. If you choose different fabrics, do the block layouts simultaneously to avoid duplication. Use the "Fabric Value Key" and strip-requirement chart accompanying each block pattern to determine the number and size of the strips and their position in the strip set.

The size and number of blocks determine the skill level. For example, it is easier to make a quilt using just one block pattern, such as "Aurora Borealis" or "Shadow Romance," than it is to make a quilt with multiple blocks.

Directions for assembling the quilts and adding borders are on pages 85–87. The finished quilt sizes reflect the addition of borders where shown.

MEDICINE MAN

by Donna Mahiger Tait, 1996, Ballwin, Missouri. Because of the combination and position of the design blocks, this quilt appears to have a central circle.

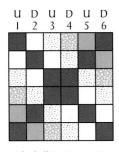

Block #1 – Queen Six
Make 4.
Strip sets on page 99.

Block #2 – Opposition
Make 4.
Strip sets on page 97.

Block #3 – Sonata
Make 8.
Strip sets on page 101.

FINISHED QUILT SIZE: 55" x 55"   ◈   BLOCK SIZES: 9", 6" x 9", 6"
SKILL LEVEL: Intermediate

Block #4 – Six Square One
Make 8.
Strip sets on page 101.

Block #5 – Six Deep A
Make 4.
Strip sets on page 101.

Block #6 – Six Deep B
Make 4.
Strip sets on page 101.

Block #7 – Six Deep C
Make 4.
Strip sets on page 101.

BLOCK DESIGN	QUEEN SIX	OPPOSITION	SONATA	SIX SQUARE ONE	SIX DEEP A & B	SIX DEEP C
Strip Size	2" x 11"	2" x 11"	2" x 20"	1½" x 20"	1½" x 18"	2" x 9"
NO. OF STRIPS						
■ Dark Dark	12	6	5	6	6	6
▨ Light Dark	0	2	7	6	10	10
▦ Dark Medium	4	4	7	6	8	8
▨ Light Medium	4	6	7	6	6	6
▫ Dark Light	8	8	7	6	4	4
□ Light Light	8	10	3	6	2	2
FROM THE ASSEMBLED STRIP SETS, CUT SEGMENTS AS FOLLOWS:						
Width	2"	2"	2"	2"	1½"	1½"
No. of Segments	4	4	8	8	4	4
Width	—	—	—	—	2"	—
No. of Segments	—	—	—	—	4	—

MATERIALS: 44"-WIDE FABRIC

- ¾ yd. for border
- ¾ yd. for binding
- 3½ yds. for backing
- 61" x 61" piece of batting

Block Construction

Refer to "Strip Piecing Your Way to a Watercolor Quilt" on pages 17–22 for information on cutting and assembling strip sets and blocks, and to the "Block Gallery" on pages 88–104 for illustrations of the strip sets required.

Crosscut strip sets as directed above and assemble the blocks shown at left.

Quilt Top Assembly

1. Arrange the blocks in 6 rows of 6 blocks each as shown in the quilt plan at right, alternating and rotating the blocks as necessary. Sew the blocks together as directed in "Assembling the Quilt Top," page 85.

•5	7•	4•	4•	6•	5•
6	1	3	3	1	7
4	3	2	2	3	4
4	3	2	2	3	4
7	1	3	3	1	6
•5	6•	4•	4•	7	5•

Dots on the quilt plan indicate the upper left corner of the design block.

2. From the border fabric, cut 6 strips, each 3¾" x 42". Cut 2 of the strips in half crosswise. Sew 1 piece to each of the 4 remaining strips, using a diagonal seam as shown on page 85.

3. Measure the quilt top for borders as described in "Borders with Straight-Cut Corners" on page 87. Trim 2 strips to fit the side edges and sew to opposite sides of the quilt top. Trim the 2 remaining strips to fit the top and bottom edges and sew to the quilt top.

4. Layer the quilt top with backing and batting; baste. Quilt as desired.

5. From the binding fabric, cut 6 strips, each 3½" x 42". Join the strips with a diagonal seam to make one piece of binding that is long enough to bind the quilt. Bind the edges, using a ½"-wide seam allowance.

BOUQUET FOR SUE

by Karen Palese, 1996, Downers Grove, Illinois. Karen's beloved daughter Sue passed away February 14, 1996, just prior to the completion of this quilt. It is lovingly dedicated to her memory.

FINISHED QUILT SIZE: 60" x 60" ❖ BLOCK SIZES: 10½ ", 7" x 10½ ", 7"
SKILL LEVEL: Intermediate

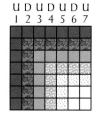

Block #1 – Seville A
Make 4.
Strip sets on page 100.

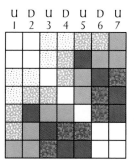

Block #2 – Seville B
Make 4.
Strip sets on page 100.

Block #3 – Barcelona
Make 12.
Strip sets on page 88.

Block #4 – King's Crown
Make 8.
Strip sets on page 94.

Block #5 – Beguile A
Make 4.
Strip sets on page 89.

Block #6 – Beguile B
Make 4.
Strip sets on page 89.

BLOCK DESIGNS	SEVILLE A	SEVILLE B	BARCELONA	KING'S CROWN	BEGUILE A	BEGUILE B
Strip Size	2" x 11"	1½" x 9"	2" x 27"	2" x 15"	2" x 9"	1½" x 11"

NO. OF STRIPS

	SEVILLE A	SEVILLE B	BARCELONA	KING'S CROWN	BEGUILE A	BEGUILE B
■ Dark Dark	13	13	8	4	19	19
▨ Light Dark	11	11	6	4	10	10
▦ Dark Medium	9	9	10	12	8	8
▥ Light Medium	7	7	8	12	6	6
▫ Dark Light	5	5	6	12	4	4
□ Light Light	4	4	11	5	2	2

FROM THE ASSEMBLED STRIP SETS, CUT SEGMENTS AS FOLLOWS:

	SEVILLE A	SEVILLE B	BARCELONA	KING'S CROWN	BEGUILE A	BEGUILE B
Width	2"	1½"	2"	1½"	1½"	2"
No. of Segments	4	4	12	8	4	4

MATERIALS: 44"-WIDE FABRIC

- ½ yd. for border
- ½ yd. for binding
- 3¾ yds. for backing
- 66" x 66" piece of batting

Block Construction

Refer to "Strip Piecing Your Way to a Watercolor Quilt" on pages 17–22 for information on cutting and assembling strip sets and blocks, and to the "Block Gallery" on pages 88–104 for illustrations of the strip sets required.

Crosscut strip sets as directed above and assemble the blocks shown at left.

Quilt Top Assembly

1. Arrange the blocks in 6 rows of 6 blocks each as shown in the quilt plan below, alternating and rotating the blocks as necessary. Sew the blocks together as directed in "Assembling the Quilt Top" on page 85.

•2	•4	•6	5 •	•4	2•
•4	1	3	3•	1 •	•4
•5	3	•3	•3	3	•6
6	3	•3	3	•3	5
•4	1	•3	3	1	•4
•2	•4	•5	6 •	•4	2•

Dots on the quilt plan indicate the upper left corner of the design block.

2. From the border fabric, cut 6 strips, each 2¼" x 42". Cut 2 of the strips in half crosswise. Sew 1 piece to each of the remaining strips, using a diagonal seam as shown on page 85.
3. Measure the quilt top for borders as described in "Borders with Straight-Cut Corners" on page 87. Trim 2 strips to fit the side edges and sew to opposite sides of the quilt top. Trim the 2 remaining strips to fit the top and bottom edges and sew to the quilt top.
4. Layer the quilt top with backing and batting; baste. Quilt as desired.
5. From the binding fabric, cut 6 strips, each 2½" x 42". Join the strips with a diagonal seam to make one piece of binding that is long enough for the quilt. Bind the edges.

CYBER COLORS TWO

by Doris Havens, 1996, Bolingbrook, Illinois. Because of the position of the light and dark values, this piece appears to include four circles even though it is pieced with strips that ultimately end up as squares. Quilted by Suzanne Barnhill.

FINISHED QUILT SIZE: 64" x 64" ❖ BLOCK SIZES: 12", 8" x 24", 8"
SKILL LEVEL: Intermediate

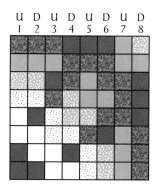

Block #1 – Mediator
Make 4.
Strip sets on page 95.

Block #2 – Act Four
Make 12.
Strip sets on page 88.

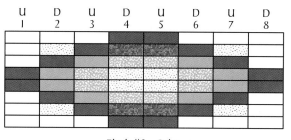

Block #3 – Ocho
Make 8.
Strip sets on page 97.

Block #4 – Unity Three
Make 4.
Strip sets on page 104.

BLOCK DESIGN	MEDIATOR	ACT FOUR	OCHO	UNITY THREE
Strip Size	2" x 11"	2" x 27"	1½" x 36"	1½" x 9"
NO. OF STRIPS				
■ Dark Dark	8	13	16	7
▨ Light Dark	10	17	4	13
▧ Dark Medium	14	12	8	11
▦ Light Medium	14	8	8	17
⬚ Dark Light	10	7	8	12
☐ Light Light	8	7	20	4
FROM THE ASSEMBLED STRIP SETS, CUT SEGMENTS AS FOLLOWS:				
Width	2"	2"	3½"	1½"
No. of Segments	4	12	8	4

MATERIALS: 44"-WIDE FABRIC

- ⅝ yd. for binding
- 4 yds. for backing
- 71" x 71" piece of batting

Block Construction

Refer to "Strip Piecing Your Way to a Watercolor Quilt" on pages 17–22 for information on cutting and assembling strip sets and blocks, and to the "Block Gallery" on pages 88–104 for illustrations of the strip sets required.

Crosscut strip sets as directed above and assemble the blocks shown at left.

Quilt Top Assembly

1. Arrange the blocks in 6 rows of 6 blocks each as shown in the quilt plan below, alternating and rotating the blocks as necessary. The 8 Ocho blocks are twice as wide as the center blocks; arrange 2 blocks on each edge of the center section, then add the 4 corner blocks.

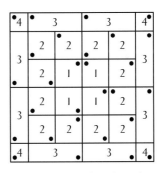

Dots on the quilt plan indicate the upper left corner of the design block.

2. Layer the quilt top with backing and batting; baste. Quilt as desired.
3. From the binding fabric, cut 7 strips, each 2½" x 42". Join the strips with a diagonal seam to make one piece of binding that is long enough for the quilt. Bind the edges.

FLYING COLORS

by Deanna Spingola, 1995, Woodridge, Illinois. Colorful illusions of fan blades originate in the center of the quilt and extend beyond to create movement. The quilting lines emphasize this energy as they continue out into the border.

FINISHED QUILT SIZE: 44½" x 44½" ❖ BLOCK SIZE: 12" ❖ SKILL LEVEL: Intermediate

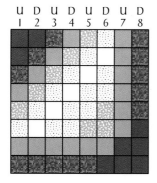

Block #1 – Corner Lot
Make 4.
Strip sets on page 90.

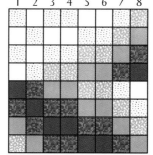

Block #2 – Positive/Negative
Make 4.
Strip sets on page 98.

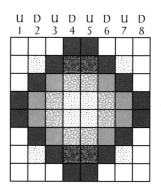

Block #3 – Ocho
Make 1.

BLOCK DESIGN	CORNER LOT	POSITIVE/NEGATIVE	OCHO
Strip Size	2" x 11"	2" x 11"	2" x 2"
NO. OF STRIPS			
■ Dark Dark	9	7	16
▨ Light Dark	13	12	4
▦ Dark Medium	16	12	8
▦ Light Medium	8	12	8
▢ Dark Light	13	13	8
□ Light Light	5	8	20
FROM THE ASSEMBLED STRIP SETS, CUT SEGMENTS AS FOLLOWS:			
Width	2"	2"	—
No. of Segments	4	4	—

MATERIALS: 44"-WIDE FABRIC

- ¼ yd. for inner border
- ½ yd. for outer border
- ½ yd. for binding
- 3 yds. for backing
- 49" x 49" piece of batting

Block Construction

Refer to "Strip Piecing Your Way to a Watercolor Quilt" on pages 17–22 for information on cutting and assembling strip sets and blocks, and to the "Block Gallery" on pages 88–104 for illustrations of the strip sets required.

Crosscut strip sets as directed above and assemble the blocks shown at left.

Quilt Top Assembly

1. Arrange the blocks in 3 rows of 3 blocks each as shown in the quilt plan below, alternating and rotating the blocks as necessary. Sew the blocks together as directed in "Assembling the Quilt Top" on page 85.

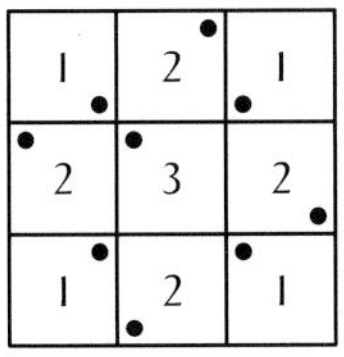

Dots on the quilt plan indicate the upper left corner of the design block.

2. From the inner border fabric, cut 6 strips, each 1½" x 44". From the outer border fabric, cut 6 strips, each 3½" x 44". Sew each inner border strip to an outer border strip. Cut 2 units in half crosswise and stitch 1 short piece to each of the 4 remaining units, using a diagonal seam as shown on page 85.

3. Measure the quilt top for borders as described in "Borders with Mitered Corners" on page 86. Trim the borders to fit and sew to the quilt top; miter the corners.

4. Layer the quilt top with backing and batting; baste. Quilt as desired.

5. From the binding fabric, cut 5 strips, each 2½" x 42". Join the strips with a diagonal seam to make one piece of binding that is long enough for the quilt. Bind the edges.

BLOCK PARTY

by Deanna Spingola, 1996, Woodridge, Illinois. The exterior rectangular blocks capture flower bouquets within their dark-value ovals. If you look closely, you'll see five flower confetti wreathes: one in each of the corners and one in the center of the quilt. Splashes of red and yellow light up the more sedate colors and are framed by a complementary border.

FINISHED QUILT SIZE: 57½" x 57½"   ⬦   BLOCK SIZES: 12", 8" x 12", 8"   ⬦   SKILL LEVEL: Intermediate

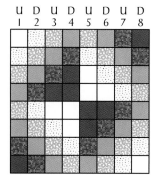

Block #1 – Mediator
Make 4.
Strip sets on page 95.

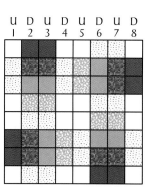

Block #2 – Eight Weave
Make 4.
Strip sets on page 92.

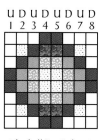

Block #3 – Ocho A
Make 4.
Strip sets on page 97.

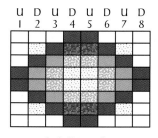

Block #4 – Ocho B
Make 12.
Strip sets on page 97.

Block Design	Mediator	Eight Weave	Ocho A & B
Strip Size	2" x 13"	2" x 11"	1½" x 33"
NO. OF STRIPS			
Dark Dark	8	8	16
Light Dark	10	8	4
Dark Medium	14	8	8
Light Medium	14	8	8
Dark Light	10	16	8
Light Light	8	16	20
FROM THE ASSEMBLED STRIP SETS, CUT SEGMENTS AS FOLLOWS:			
Width	2"	2"	1½"
No. of Segments	5	4	4
Width	—	—	2"
No. of Segments	—	—	12

MATERIALS: 44"-WIDE FABRIC

- ⅝ yd. for border
- ½ yd. for binding
- 3½ yds. for backing
- 62" x 62" piece of batting

Block Construction

✄ Note ✄

The weave blocks require special attention to ensure that the visual illusion of the over-and-under weave is carried through the block. The following steps will help you achieve this goal.

1. Make sure 1½" of each fabric is showing for a clear view of the block you are constructing.
2. Check the values to make sure the dark-dark fabrics are evenly dark on both sides of the lighter strips. Use a reducing tool or the Ruby Beholder to check the values.
3. Stand back from the strips after you lay them out and make sure you can see the weave.

Refer to "Strip Piecing Your Way to a Watercolor Quilt" on pages 17–22 for information on cutting and assembling strip sets and blocks, and to the "Block Gallery" on pages 88–104 for illustrations of the strip sets required.

Crosscut strip sets as directed above and assemble the blocks shown at left.

Quilt Top Assembly

1. Arrange the blocks in 5 rows of 5 blocks each as shown in the quilt plan at right, alternating and rotating the blocks as necessary. Sew the blocks together as directed in "Assembling the Quilt Top" on page 85.

•3	•4	•4	•4	•3
4•	•1	•2	•1	4
4•	•2	•1	•2	4
4•	•1	•2	•1	4
•3	•4	•4	•4	•3

Dots on the quilt plan indicate the upper left corner of the design block.

2. From the border fabric, cut 6 strips, each 3" x 42". Cut 2 of the strips in half crosswise and sew 1 piece to each of the 4 remaining strips, using a diagonal seam as shown on page 85.
3. Measure the quilt top for borders as described in "Borders with Mitered Corners" on page 86. Trim the borders to fit and sew to the quilt top; miter the corners.
4. Layer the quilt top with backing and batting; baste. Quilt as desired.
5. From the binding fabric, cut 6 strips, each 2½" x 42". Join the strips with a diagonal seam to make one piece of binding that is long enough for the quilt. Bind the edges.

SUNRISE SERENADE

by Deanna Spingola, 1995, Woodridge, Illinois. The position of light and dark values in the paper-pieced border produces the illusion of curves on the edges of this quilt. To accentuate the illusion of the circle, make sure you choose dark-dark values where the pattern calls for it.

FINISHED QUILT SIZE: 48" x 48" ◈ BLOCK SIZES: 12", 6" ◈ SKILL LEVEL: Advanced

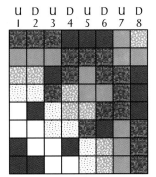

Block #1 – Act Four
Make 4.
Strip sets on page 88.

Block #2 – Eight Weave
Make 4.
Strip sets on page 92.

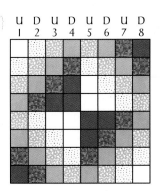

Block #3 – Mediator
Make 1.

Block #4 – Sunrise
Make 28.
Foundation on page 105.

BLOCK DESIGN		ACT FOUR	EIGHT WEAVE	MEDIATOR	SUNRISE
Strip Size		2" x 11"	2" x 11"	2" x 2"	1¾" x 6½"
NO. OF STRIPS					
■	Dark Dark	13	8	8	84
▨	Light Dark	17	8	10	84
▦	Dark Medium	12	8	14	84
▨	Light Medium	8	8	14	84
⬚	Dark Light	7	16	10	112
☐	Light Light	7	16	8	56
FROM THE ASSEMBLED STRIP SETS, CUT SEGMENTS AS FOLLOWS:					
Width		2"	2"	—	—
No. of Segments		4	4	—	—

MATERIALS: 44"-WIDE FABRIC

- ½ yd. for binding
- 3 yds. for backing
- 54" x 54" piece of batting

Block Construction

Refer to "Strip Piecing Your Way to a Watercolor Quilt" on pages 17–22 for information on cutting and assembling strip sets and blocks, and to the "Block Gallery" on pages 88–104 for illustrations of the strip sets required.

Crosscut strip sets as directed above and assemble the blocks shown at left.

Because paper-pieced blocks are exact, the blocks you make from strip sets must be accurate so all the blocks fit together. Refer to "Foundation Paper Piecing" on page 84 to make 28 Sunrise blocks for the border. Use the paper foundation pattern on page 105.

Quilt Top Assembly

1. Arrange the 9 center blocks in 3 rows of 3 blocks each as shown in the quilt plan at right, alternating and rotating the blocks as necessary. Sew them together as directed in "Assembling the Quilt Top," page 85.

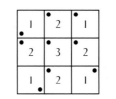

Dots on the quilt plan indicate the upper left corner of the design block.

2. Arrange 6 border blocks as shown and sew them together to make 2 side borders.

3. Arrange 8 border blocks as shown and sew them together to make 2 top and bottom borders.

4. Sew the side borders to opposite side edges of the quilt top; add the top and bottom borders.

5. Layer the quilt top with backing and batting; baste. Quilt as desired.
6. From the binding fabric, cut 5 strips, each 2½" x 42". Join the strips with a diagonal seam to make one piece of binding that is long enough for the quilt. Bind the edges.

$\mathscr{T}$HE BOUQUET

by Carol Schertz Deal, 1996, Bloomington, Illinois. This lovely wall hanging features a basket filled with dimensional-fabric and ribbon flowers. It is stippled throughout for additional texture.

FINISHED QUILT SIZE: 33" x 33"   ◈   BLOCK SIZE: 13½"   ◈   SKILL LEVEL: Intermediate

Block #1 – Wicker
Make 2.
Strip sets on page 104.

Block #2 – Handle
Make 2.
Strip sets on page 93.

BLOCK DESIGN	WICKER	HANDLE
Strip Size	2" x 6"	2" x 6"
NO. OF STRIPS		
▪ Dark Dark	27	12
▪ Light Dark	4	20
▫ Dark Medium	7	15
▫ Light Medium	19	11
▫ Dark Light	18	15
▫ Light Light	6	8

FROM THE ASSEMBLED STRIP SETS,
CUT SEGMENTS AS FOLLOWS:

Width	2"	2"
No. of Segments	2	2

- Assorted scraps for appliqués
- ½ yd. for border
- ⅜ yd. for binding
- 1⅛ yds. for backing
- 38" x 38" piece of batting

Block Construction

Refer to "Strip Piecing Your Way to a Watercolor Quilt" on pages 17–22 for information on cutting and assembling strip sets and blocks, and to the "Block Gallery" on pages 88–104 for illustrations of the strip sets required.

Crosscut strip sets as directed above and assemble the blocks shown at left.

Quilt Top Assembly

1. Arrange the blocks in 2 rows of 2 blocks each as shown in the quilt plan below, alternating and rotating the blocks as necessary. Sew the blocks together as directed in "Assembling the Quilt Top" on page 85.

Dots on the quilt plan indicate the
upper left corner of the design block.

2. Cut appliqué pieces using the template patterns on page 104. Cut the leaves and flowers from a variety of solid-colored fabrics. Using your favorite method, appliqué the flowers and leaves to the center of the quilt top. Refer to the quilt photo at left for placement. See "Appliqué" on page 84.

3. From the border fabric, cut 4 strips, each 3¼" x 42". Measure the quilt top for borders as described in "Borders with Straight-Cut Corners" on page 87. Trim 2 strips to fit the side edges and sew to opposite sides of the quilt top. Trim the 2 remaining strips to fit the top and bottom edges and sew to the quilt top.

4. Layer the quilt top with backing and batting; baste. Quilt as desired.

5. From the binding fabric, cut 4 strips, each 2½" x 42". Join the strips with a diagonal seam to make one piece of binding that is long enough for the quilt. Bind the edges.

 MAZED *by Barbara Wessel, 1996, Deerfield, Illinois. Barbara was amazed that all those busy, colorful fabrics would come together and create such a stunning quilt.*

FINISHED QUILT SIZE: 65½" x 65½" ✦ BLOCK SIZE: 13½" ✦ SKILL LEVEL: Intermediate

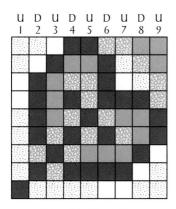

Block #1 – Hearts Two
Make 4.
Strip sets on page 94.

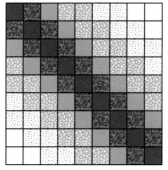

Block #2 – Dark Line
Make 4.
Strip sets on page 91.

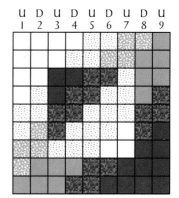

Block #3 – Square Square
Make 8.
Strip sets on page 102.

BLOCK DESIGN	HEARTS TWO	DARK LINE	SQUARE SQUARE
Strip Size	2" x 11"	2" x 11"	2" x 20"

NO. OF STRIPS

		HEARTS TWO	DARK LINE	SQUARE SQUARE
■	Dark Dark	26	9	13
▨	Light Dark	0	16	15
▢	Dark Medium	14	14	12
▨	Light Medium	16	22	8
▫	Dark Light	16	14	20
☐	Light Light	9	6	13

FROM THE ASSEMBLED STRIP SETS, CUT SEGMENTS AS FOLLOWS:

	HEARTS TWO	DARK LINE	SQUARE SQUARE
Width	2"	2"	2"
No. of Segments	4	4	8

MATERIALS: 44"-WIDE FABRIC

- ¼ yd. for inner border
- 160 leftover 2" squares from strip sets for middle border
- ¾ yd. for outer border
- ⅝ yd. for binding
- 4 yds. for backing
- 72" x 72" piece of batting

Block Construction

Refer to "Strip Piecing Your Way to a Watercolor Quilt" on pages 17–22 for information on cutting and assembling strip sets and blocks, and to the "Block Gallery" on pages 88–104 for illustrations of the strip sets required.

Crosscut strip sets as directed above and assemble the blocks shown at left.

Quilt Top Assembly

1. Arrange the blocks in 4 rows of 4 blocks as shown in the quilt plan below, alternating and rotating the blocks as necessary. Sew the blocks together as directed in "Assembling the Quilt Top" on page 85.

I	3	3	I
3	2	2	3
3	2	2	3
I	3	3	I

Dots on the quilt plan indicate the upper left corner of the design block.

2. From the inner border fabric, cut 6 strips, each 1¼" x 42". Cut 2 of the strips in half crosswise and sew 1 piece to each of the 4 remaining strips, using a diagonal seam as shown on page 85.

3. Measure the quilt top for borders as described in "Borders with Straight-Cut Corners" on page 87. Trim 2 strips to fit the side edges and sew to opposite sides of the quilt top. Trim the 2 remaining strips to fit the top and bottom edges and sew to the quilt top.

4. Using the 160 leftover 2" squares from the strip sets, make 4 border strips of 40 squares each. Arrange the squares from darkest in the center of the strips to lightest at the ends. Trim 2 strips to fit the side edges, keeping the dark squares centered, and sew to opposite sides of the quilt top. Trim the 2 remaining strips to fit the top and bottom edges, keeping the dark squares centered, and sew to the quilt top.

5. From the outer border fabric, cut 6 strips, each 3¾" x 42". Cut 2 of the strips in half crosswise and sew 1 piece to each of the 4 remaining strips, using a diagonal seam. Measure, trim, and sew the strips to the quilt top as you did for the inner border.

6. Layer the quilt top with backing and batting; baste. Quilt as desired.

7. From the binding fabric, cut 7 strips, each 2½" x 42". Join the strips with a diagonal seam to make one piece of binding that is long enough for the quilt. Bind the edges.

ENDOWMENT

by Deanna Spingola, 1995, Woodridge, Illinois. The middle of this quilt is highlighted by the light values that create an interesting relationship with the pattern of the darker center. Quilted by Gerri Buchholz.

FINISHED QUILT SIZE: 66½" x 66½" ◈ BLOCK SIZE: 15" ◈ SKILL LEVEL: Intermediate

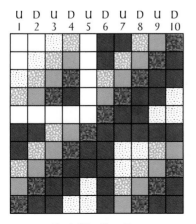

Block #1 – Sioux Two
Make 8.
Strip sets on page 100.

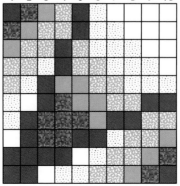

Block #2 – Tops
Make 4.
Strip sets on page 102.

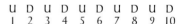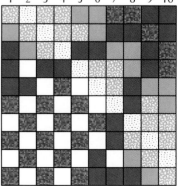

Block #3 – St. Charles
Make 4.
Strip sets on page 99.

BLOCK DESIGN	SIOUX TWO	TOPS	ST. CHARLES
Strip Size	2" x 20"	2" x 11"	2" x 11"

NO. OF STRIPS

	SIOUX TWO	TOPS	ST. CHARLES
■ Dark Dark	33	22	23
▨ Light Dark	15	10	20
▢ Dark Medium	13	11	13
▦ Light Medium	15	23	17
▢ Dark Light	12	20	9
▢ Light Light	12	14	18

FROM THE ASSEMBLED STRIP SETS, CUT SEGMENTS AS FOLLOWS:

	SIOUX TWO	TOPS	ST. CHARLES
Width	2"	2"	2"
No. of Segments	8	4	4

MATERIALS: 44"-WIDE FABRIC

- ⅞ yd. for border
- ⅝ yd. for binding
- 4 yds. for backing
- 71" x 71" piece of batting

Block Construction

Refer to "Strip Piecing Your Way to a Watercolor Quilt" on pages 17–22 for information on cutting and assembling strip sets and blocks, and to the "Block Gallery" on pages 88–104 for illustrations of the strip sets required.

Crosscut strip sets as directed above and assemble the blocks shown at left.

Quilt Top Assembly

1. Arrange the blocks in 4 rows of 4 blocks each as shown in the quilt plan below, alternating and rotating the blocks as necessary. Sew the blocks together as directed in "Assembling the Quilt Top" on page 85.

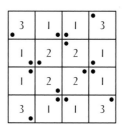

Dots on the quilt plan indicate the
upper left corner of the design block.

2. From the border fabric, cut 8 strips, each 3½" x 42". Join pairs of strips with a diagonal seam as shown on page 85.
3. Measure the quilt top for borders as described in "Borders with Mitered Corners" on page 86. Trim the borders to fit and sew to the quilt top; miter the corners.
4. Layer the quilt top with backing and batting; baste. Quilt as desired.
5. From the binding fabric, cut 7 strips, each 2½" x 42". Join the strips with a diagonal seam to make one piece of binding that is long enough for the quilt. Bind the edges.

DECK THE HALLS

by Deanna Spingola, 1995, Woodridge, Illinois. The busy colors and design provide a foundation for the intricate quilting design created by Quilt Acclaim of Leland, Illinois.

FINISHED QUILT SIZE: 67½" x 67½"   ◈   BLOCK SIZE: 15"   ◈   SKILL LEVEL: Beginner

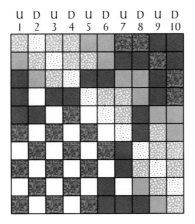

Block #1 – St. Charles
Make 4.
Strip sets on page 99.

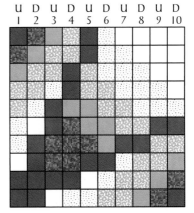

Block #2 – Tops
Make 12.
Strip sets on page 102.

BLOCK DESIGN	ST. CHARLES	TOPS
Strip Size	2" x 11"	2" x 27"

NO. OF STRIPS

	BLOCK DESIGN	ST. CHARLES	TOPS
■	Dark Dark	23	22
▨	Light Dark	20	10
▦	Dark Medium	13	11
▧	Light Medium	17	23
▫	Dark Light	9	20
□	Light Light	18	14

FROM THE ASSEMBLED STRIP SETS,

CUT SEGMENTS AS FOLLOWS:

	ST. CHARLES	TOPS
Width	2"	2"
No. of Segments	4	12

MATERIALS: 44"-WIDE FABRIC

- 1 yd. for border
- ⅝ yd. for binding
- 4 yds. for backing
- 72" x 72" piece of batting

Block Construction

Refer to "Strip Piecing Your Way to a Watercolor Quilt" on pages 17–22 for information on cutting and assembling strip sets and blocks, and to the "Block Gallery" on pages 88–104 for illustrations of the strip sets required.

Crosscut strip sets as directed above and assemble the blocks shown at left.

Quilt Top Assembly

1. Arrange the blocks in 4 rows of 4 blocks each as shown in the quilt plan below, alternating and rotating the blocks as necessary. Join the blocks as directed in "Assembling the Quilt Top" on page 85.

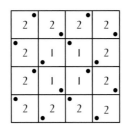

Dots on the quilt plan indicate the upper left corner of the design block.

2. From the border fabric, cut 8 strips, each 4" x 42". Join pairs of strips with a diagonal seam as shown on page 85.
3. Measure the quilt top for borders as described in "Borders with Mitered Corners" on page 86. Trim the borders to fit and sew to the quilt top; miter the corners.
4. Layer the quilt top with backing and batting; baste. Quilt as desired.
5. From the binding fabric, cut 7 strips, each 2½" x 42". Join the strips with a diagonal seam to make one piece of binding that is long enough for the quilt. Bind the edges.

ANTHONY'S STAR

by Deanna Spingola, 1995, Woodridge, Illinois. Colors radiating from the center create a stunning star design. Quilted by Quilt Acclaim.

FINISHED QUILT SIZE: 52½" x 52½" ✦ BLOCK SIZE: 15" ✦ SKILL LEVEL: Intermediate

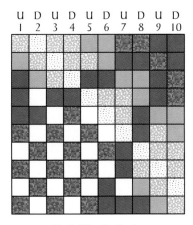

Block #1 – St. Charles
Make 4.
Strip sets on page 99.

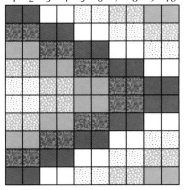

Block #2 – Dark Arrow
Make 4.
Strip sets on page 91.

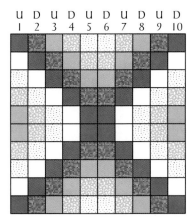

Block #3 – Toltec
Make 1.

BLOCK DESIGN	ST. CHARLES	DARK ARROW	TOLTEC
Strip Size	2" x 11"	2" x 11"	2" x 2"

NO. OF STRIPS

	ST. CHARLES	DARK ARROW	TOLTEC
▪ Dark Dark	23	20	20
▪ Light Dark	20	16	16
▪ Dark Medium	13	16	16
▪ Light Medium	17	16	16
▪ Dark Light	9	16	16
▪ Light Light	18	16	16

FROM THE ASSEMBLED STRIP SETS, CUT SEGMENTS AS FOLLOWS:

	ST. CHARLES	DARK ARROW	TOLTEC
Width	2"	2"	—
No. of Segments	4	4	—

MATERIALS: 44"-WIDE FABRIC

- ⅓ yd. for inner border
- ⅝ yd. for outer border
- ⅝ yd. for binding
- 3¼ yds. for backing
- 59" x 59" piece of batting

Block Construction

Refer to "Strip Piecing Your Way to a Watercolor Quilt" on pages 17–22 for information on cutting and assembling strip sets and blocks, and to the "Block Gallery" on pages 88–104 for illustrations of the strip sets required.

Crosscut strip sets as directed above and assemble the blocks shown at left.

Quilt Top Assembly

1. Arrange the blocks in 3 rows of 3 blocks each as shown in the quilt plan below, alternating and rotating the blocks as necessary. Sew the blocks together as directed in "Assembling the Quilt Top" on page 85.

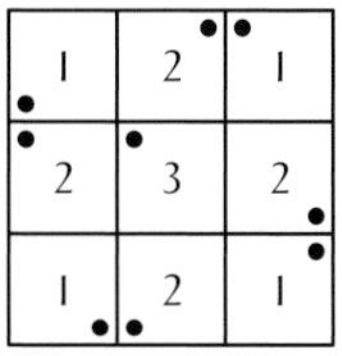

Dots on the quilt plan indicate the
upper left corner of the design block.

2. From the inner border fabric, cut 6 strips, each 1½" x 42". From the outer border fabric, cut 6 strips, each 3" x 42". Sew the inner and outer border strips together. Cut 2 of the units in half crosswise and sew 1 piece to each of the 4 remaining units, using a diagonal seam as shown on page 85.

3. Measure the quilt top for borders as described in "Borders with Mitered Corners" on page 86. Trim the borders to fit and sew to the quilt top; miter the corners.

4. Layer the quilt top with backing and batting; baste. Quilt as desired.

5. From the binding fabric, cut 6 strips, each 3½" x 42". Join the strips with a diagonal seam to make one piece of binding that is long enough to bind the quilt. Bind the edges, using a ½"-wide seam allowance.

CENTRO THREE

by Carol Sherwood, 1996, Bolingbrook, Illinois. Another arrangement of the same blocks that were used in "Anthony's Star" on page 44 result in this four-point star design.

FINISHED QUILT SIZE: 51½" x 51½" ⬦ BLOCK SIZE: 15" ⬦ SKILL LEVEL: Intermediate

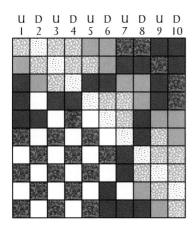

Block #1 – St. Charles
Make 4.
Strip sets on page 99.

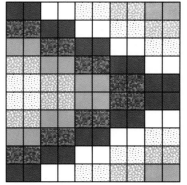

Block #2 – Dark Arrow
Make 4.
Strip sets on page 91.

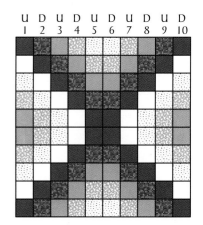

Block #3 – Toltec
Make 1.

BLOCK DESIGN	ST. CHARLES	DARK ARROW	TOLTEC
Strip Size	2" x 11"	2" x 11"	2" x 2"
NO. OF STRIPS			
Dark Dark	23	20	20
Light Dark	20	16	16
Dark Medium	13	16	16
Light Medium	17	16	16
Dark Light	9	16	16
Light Light	18	16	16
FROM THE ASSEMBLED STRIP SETS, CUT SEGMENTS AS FOLLOWS:			
Width	2"	2"	—
No. of Segments	4	4	—

MATERIALS: 44"-WIDE FABRIC

- ¾ yd. for border
- ½ yd. for binding
- 3¼ yds. for backing
- 58" x 58" piece of batting

Block Construction

Refer to "Strip Piecing Your Way to a Watercolor Quilt" on pages 17–22 for information on cutting and assembling strip sets and blocks, and to the "Block Gallery" on pages 88–104 for illustrations of the strip sets required.

Crosscut strip sets as directed above and assemble the blocks shown at left.

Quilt Top Assembly

1. Arrange the blocks in 3 rows of 3 blocks each as shown in the quilt plan below, alternating and rotating the blocks as necessary. Sew the blocks together as directed in "Assembling the Quilt Top" on page 85.

Dots on the quilt plan indicate the upper left corner of the design block.

2. From the border fabric, cut 6 strips, each 3½" x 42". Cut 2 of the strips in half crosswise and sew 1 piece to each of the 4 remaining strips, using a diagonal seam as shown on page 85.
3. Measure the quilt top for borders as described in "Borders with Straight-Cut Corners" on page 87. Trim 2 border strips to fit opposite side edges and sew to the sides of the quilt top. Trim the 2 remaining strips to fit the top and bottom edges and sew to the quilt top.
4. Layer the quilt top with backing and batting; baste. Quilt as desired.
5. From the binding fabric, cut 6 strips, each 2½" x 42". Join the strips with a diagonal seam to make one piece of binding that is long enough for the quilt. Bind the edges.

Be My Valentine

by Tracey Steinbach, 1996, Downers Grove, Illinois. Tracey designed an initial block for the center of this quilt and surrounded it with creative appliqué to draw attention to it.

FINISHED QUILT SIZE: 53" x 53" ◈ BLOCK SIZE: 15" ◈ SKILL LEVEL: Intermediate

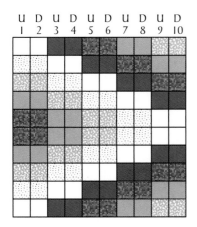

U	D	U	D	U	D	U	D	U	D
1	2	3	4	5	6	7	8	9	10

Block #1 – Light Arrow
Make 4.
Strip sets on page 94.

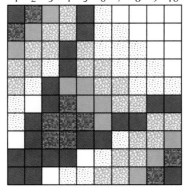

U	D	U	D	U	D	U	D	U	D
1	2	3	4	5	6	7	8	9	10

Block #2 – Tops
Make 4.
Strip sets on page 102.

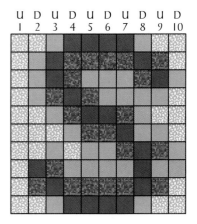

U	D	U	D	U	D	U	D	U	D
1	2	3	4	5	6	7	8	9	10

Block #3 – ESS2
Make 1.

BLOCK DESIGN	LIGHT ARROW	TOPS	ESS2
Strip Size	2" x 11"	2" x 11"	2" x 2"

NO. OF STRIPS

		LIGHT ARROW	TOPS	ESS2
■	Dark Dark	16	22	21
▨	Light Dark	16	10	22
▦	Dark Medium	16	11	30
▦	Light Medium	16	23	27
▢	Dark Light	16	20	0
□	Light Light	20	14	0

FROM THE ASSEMBLED STRIP SETS, CUT SEGMENTS AS FOLLOWS:

	LIGHT ARROW	TOPS	ESS2
Width	2"	2"	—
No. of Segments	4	4	—

MATERIALS: 44"-WIDE FABRIC

- ⅜ yd. rose print for appliqué
- ⅓ yd. for inner border
- ⅝ yd. for outer border
- ⅝ yd. for binding
- 3¼ yds. for backing
- 59" x 59" piece of batting

Block Construction

Refer to "Strip Piecing Your Way to a Watercolor Quilt" on pages 17–22 for information on cutting and assembling strip sets and blocks, and to the "Block Gallery" on pages 88–104 for illustrations of the strip sets required.

Crosscut strip sets as directed above and assemble the blocks shown at left.

Quilt Top Assembly

1. Arrange the blocks in 3 rows of 3 blocks each as shown in the quilt plan below, alternating and rotating the blocks as necessary. Sew the blocks together as directed in "Assembling the Quilt Top" on page 85.

```
┌───┬───┬───┐
│2 •│ 1 │2 •│
│   │•  │   │
├───┼───┼───┤
│ 1 │ 3 │ 1 │
│  •│   │   │
├───┼───┼───┤
│•  │ 1 │•  │
│2  │  •│2  │
└───┴───┴───┘
```

Dots on the quilt plan indicate the
upper left corner of the design block.

2. From the inner border fabric, cut 6 strips, each 1½" x 42". Cut 2 of the strips in half crosswise and sew 1 piece to each of the 4 remaining strips, using a diagonal seam as shown on page 85.

3. From the outer border fabric, cut 6 strips, each 3¼" x 42". Cut 2 of the strips in half crosswise and sew 1 piece to each of the 4 remaining strips, using a diagonal seam.

4. Measure the quilt top for borders as described in "Borders with Straight-Cut Corners" on page 87. Trim 2 inner border strips to fit the side edges and sew to opposite sides of the quilt top. Trim the 2 remaining strips to fit the top and bottom edges and sew to the quilt top. Add the outer borders in the same manner.

5. Make appliqué pieces using the template pattern on page 106. To have 5 left-facing pieces and 5 right-facing pieces, fold the fabric in half, wrong sides together; trace the pattern 5 times on the top layer of fabric. Cut out both layers. Using your favorite method, appliqué the designs to the quilt top. Refer to the quilt photo for placement. See "Appliqué" on page 84.

6. Layer the quilt top with backing and batting; baste. Quilt as desired.

7. From the binding fabric, cut 6 strips, each 2½" x 42". Join the strips with a diagonal seam to make one piece of binding that is long enough for the quilt. Bind the edges.

A WORLD OF HOPE AND DREAMS

by Susan L. Harmon, 1996, Naperville, Illinois. Lights, checkered darks, twirling fans, and the illusion of a circle in the center make this quilt a conversation piece.

FINISHED QUILT SIZE: 60" x 60"   ✧   BLOCK SIZE: 15"   ✧   SKILL LEVEL: Intermediate

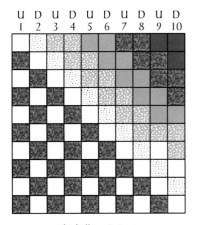

Block #1 – St. Louis
Make 4.
Strip sets on page 100.

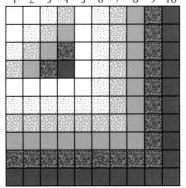

Block #2 – Midnight
Make 4.
Strip sets on page 96.

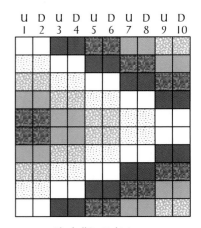

Block #3 – Light Arrow
Make 8.
Strip sets on page 94.

BLOCK DESIGN	ST. LOUIS	MIDNIGHT	LIGHT ARROW
Strip Size	2" x 11"	2" x 11"	2" x 20"
NO. OF STRIPS			
■ Dark Dark	3	20	16
▨ Light Dark	32	19	16
▨ Dark Medium	11	18	16
▨ Light Medium	15	17	16
▨ Dark Light	9	14	16
□ Light Light	30	12	20
FROM THE ASSEMBLED STRIP SETS, CUT SEGMENTS AS FOLLOWS:			
Width	2"	2"	2"
No. of Segments	4	4	8

MATERIALS: 44"-WIDE FABRIC

- ½ yd. for binding
- 3⅞ yds. for backing
- 66" x 66" piece of batting

Block Construction

Refer to "Strip Piecing Your Way to a Watercolor Quilt" on pages 17–22 for information on cutting and assembling strip sets and blocks, and to the "Block Gallery" on pages 88–104 for illustrations of the strip sets required.

Crosscut strip sets as directed above and assemble the blocks shown at left.

Quilt Top Assembly

1. Arrange the blocks in 4 rows of 4 blocks each as shown in the quilt plan below, alternating and rotating the blocks as necessary. Sew the blocks together as directed in "Assembling the Quilt Top" on page 85.

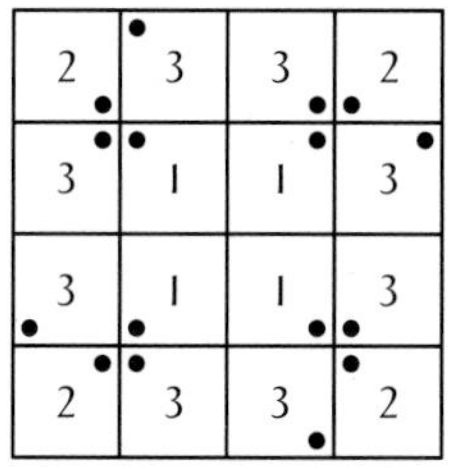

2	3	3	2
3	1	1	3
3	1	1	3
2	3	3	2

Dots on the quilt plan indicate the
upper left corner of the design block.

2. Layer the quilt top with backing and batting; baste. Quilt as desired.
3. From the binding fabric, cut 6 strips, each 2½" x 42". Join the strips with a diagonal seam to make one piece of binding that is long enough for the quilt. Bind the edges.

by Pam Bryon, 1996, Ballwin, Missouri. An interesting diamond-shaped center, circled with light values and accented with attractive dark- to light-value corners, make this an engaging quilt.

FINISHED QUILT SIZE: 60" x 60" ❖ BLOCK SIZES: 15", 15" x 10", 10" ❖ SKILL LEVEL: Intermediate

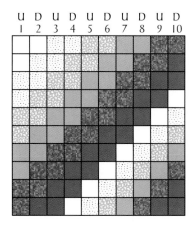

Block #1 – Nevada
Make 4.
Strip sets on page 96.

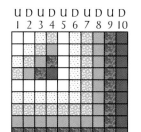

Block #2 – Midnight
Make 4.
Strip sets on page 96.

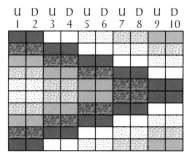

Block #3 – Dark Arrow
Make 8.
Strip sets on page 91.

Block Design	Nevada	Midnight	Dark Arrow
Strip Size	2" x 11"	1½" x 9"	1½" x 20"

NO. OF STRIPS

	Nevada	Midnight	Dark Arrow
◼ Dark Dark	20	20	20
▨ Light Dark	22	19	16
▧ Dark Medium	19	18	16
▨ Light Medium	16	17	16
▫ Dark Light	13	14	16
◻ Light Light	10	12	16

FROM THE ASSEMBLED STRIP SETS, CUT SEGMENTS AS FOLLOWS:

Width	2"	1½"	2"
No. of Segments	4	4	8

MATERIALS: 44"-WIDE FABRIC

- ⅓ yd. for inner border
- ¾ yd. for outer border
- ½ yd. for binding
- 3¾ yds. for backing
- 66" x 66" piece of batting

Block Construction

Refer to "Strip Piecing Your Way to a Watercolor Quilt" on pages 17–22 for information on cutting and assembling strip sets and blocks, and to the "Block Gallery" on pages 88–104 for illustrations of the strip sets required.

Crosscut strip sets as directed above and assemble the blocks shown at left.

Quilt Top Assembly

1. Arrange the blocks in 4 rows of 4 blocks each as shown in the quilt plan below, alternating and rotating the blocks as necessary. Sew the blocks together as directed in "Assembling the Quilt Top" on page 85.

Dots on the quilt plan indicate the upper left corner of the design block.

2. From the inner border fabric, cut 6 strips, each 1½" x 42". Cut 2 of the strips in half crosswise and sew 1 piece to each of the 4 remaining strips, using a diagonal seam as shown on page 85.

3. Measure the quilt top for borders as described in "Borders with Straight-Cut Corners" on page 87. Trim 2 strips to fit the side edges and sew to opposite sides of the quilt top. Trim the 2 remaining strips to fit the top and bottom edges and sew to the quilt top.

4. From the outer border fabric, cut 6 strips, each 4¼" x 42". Cut 2 of the strips in half crosswise and sew 1 piece to each of the 4 remaining strips, using a diagonal seam.

5. Measure, trim, and add the outer borders as you did the inner borders.

6. Layer the quilt top with backing and batting; baste. Quilt as desired.

7. From the binding fabric, cut 6 strips, each 2½" x 42". Join the strips with a diagonal seam to make one piece of binding that is long enough for the quilt. Bind the edges.

TWIN PEAKS

by Marilyn Leccese, 1996, Ankeny, Iowa. Checkered corners and dark-value peaks are the highlight of this large bed-size quilt. Who said you couldn't easily create a beautiful bed-size watercolor quilt?

FINISHED QUILT SIZE: 84" x 114" ◈ BLOCK SIZE: 15" ◈ SKILL LEVEL: Intermediate

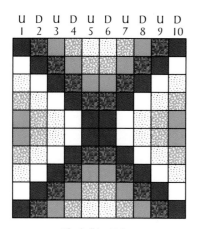

Block #1 – Toltec
Make 9.
Strip sets on page 102.

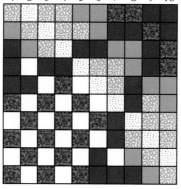

Block #2 – St. Charles
Make 12.
Strip sets on page 99.

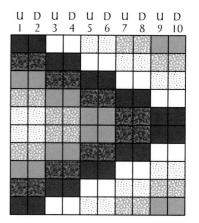

Block #3 – Dark Arrow
Make 14.
Strip sets on page 91.

BLOCK DESIGN	TOLTEC	ST. CHARLES	DARK ARROW
Strip Size	2" x 22"	2" x 27"	2" x 31"

NO. OF STRIPS

	TOLTEC	ST. CHARLES	DARK ARROW
Dark Dark	20	23	20
Light Dark	16	20	16
Dark Medium	16	13	16
Light Medium	16	17	16
Dark Light	16	9	16
Light Light	16	18	16

FROM THE ASSEMBLED STRIP SETS, CUT SEGMENTS AS FOLLOWS:

	TOLTEC	ST. CHARLES	DARK ARROW
Width	2"	2"	2"
No. of Segments	9	12	14

MATERIALS: 44"-WIDE FABRIC

- 1½ yds. for border
- ¾ yd. for binding
- 6¾ yds. for backing
- 90" x 120" piece of batting

Block Construction

Refer to "Strip Piecing Your Way to a Watercolor Quilt" on pages 17–22 for information on cutting and assembling strip sets and blocks, and to the "Block Gallery" on pages 88–104 for illustrations of the strip sets required.

Crosscut strip sets as directed above and assemble the blocks shown at left.

Quilt Top Assembly

1. Arrange the blocks in 7 rows of 5 blocks each as shown in the quilt plan at right, alternating and rotating the blocks as necessary. Sew the blocks together as directed in "Assembling the Quilt Top" on page 85.

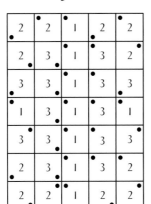

2	2	1	2	2
2	3	1	3	2
3	3	1	3	3
1	3	1	3	1
3	3	1	3	3
2	3	1	3	2
2	2	1	2	2

Dots on the quilt plan indicate the upper left corner of the design block.

Note
The maker chose two different prints for the borders of this quilt.

2. From the border fabric, cut 11 strips, each 4¾" x 42". For each side border, sew 3 of the strips together, using a diagonal seam as shown on page 85. Cut 1 of the remaining strips in half crosswise; sew 2 full strips and 1 half strip together for each of the top and bottom borders.

Side Borders
Make 2.

Top and Bottom Borders
Make 2.

3. Measure the quilt top for borders as described in "Borders with Mitered Corners" on page 86. Trim the borders to fit and sew to the quilt top; miter the corners.
4. Layer the quilt top with backing and batting; baste. Quilt as desired.
5. From the binding fabric, cut 10 strips, each 2½" x 42". Join the strips with a diagonal seam to make one piece of binding that is long enough for the quilt. Bind the edges.

DREAMING OF PARIS

by Nancy Bolliger, 1996, Naperville, Illinois. An exploration of Paris, a significant travel event, is the inspiration for the name of this wonderful quilt that explores emerging shapes and values.

FINISHED QUILT SIZE: 63½" x 63½" ◈ BLOCK SIZES: 15", 10" x 15", 10" ◈ SKILL LEVEL: Intermediate

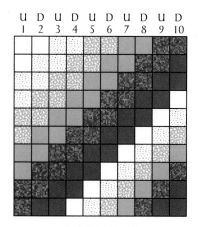

Block #1 – Nevada
Make 4.
Strip sets on page 96.

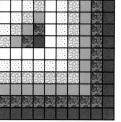

Block #2 – Midnight
Make 4.
Strip sets on page 96.

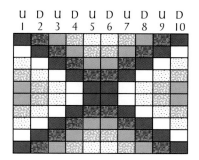

Block #3 – Toltec
Make 8.
Strip sets on page 102.

BLOCK DESIGN	NEVADA	MIDNIGHT	TOLTEC
Strip Size	2" x 11"	1½" x 9"	1½" x 20"

NO. OF STRIPS

	NEVADA	MIDNIGHT	TOLTEC
■ Dark Dark	17	20	20
▨ Light Dark	22	19	16
▦ Dark Medium	19	18	16
▨ Light Medium	16	17	16
▫ Dark Light	13	14	16
□ Light Light	10	12	16

FROM THE ASSEMBLED STRIP SETS, CUT SEGMENTS AS FOLLOWS:

	NEVADA	MIDNIGHT	TOLTEC
Width	2"	1½"	2"
No. of Segments	4	4	8

MATERIALS: 44"-WIDE FABRIC

- 2 yds. for border
- ⅝ yd. for binding
- 3⅞ yds. for backing
- 68" x 68" piece of batting

Block Construction

Refer to "Strip Piecing Your Way to a Watercolor Quilt" on pages 17–22 for information on cutting and assembling strip sets and blocks, and to the "Block Gallery" on pages 88–104 for illustrations of the strip sets required.

Crosscut strip sets as directed above and assemble the blocks shown at left.

Quilt Top Assembly

1. Arrange the blocks in 4 rows of 4 blocks each as shown in the quilt plan below, alternating and rotating the blocks as necessary. Sew the blocks together as directed in "Assembling the Quilt Top" on page 85.

Dots on the quilt plan indicate the
upper left corner of the design block.

2. From the lengthwise grain of the border fabric, cut 4 strips, each 7" x 72".
3. Measure the quilt top for borders as described in "Borders with Straight-Cut Corners" on page 87. Trim 2 strips to fit the side edges and sew to opposite sides of the quilt top. Trim the 2 remaining strips to fit the top and bottom edges and sew to the quilt top.
4. Layer the quilt top with backing and batting; baste. Quilt as desired.
5. From the binding fabric, cut 6 strips, each 3½" x 42". Join the strips with a diagonal seam to make one piece of binding that is long enough to bind the quilt. Bind the edges, using a ½"-wide seam allowance.

SUMMER SYMPHONY

by Deanna Spingola, 1996, Woodridge, Illinois. The pure, warm hues of summer create the symphony of color, while definitive value changes cascade across the surface of this quilt. Heavy stipple quilting adds great texture and interest.

FINISHED QUILT SIZE: 74" x 74"   ◈   BLOCK SIZE: 16½"   ◈   SKILL LEVEL: Intermediate

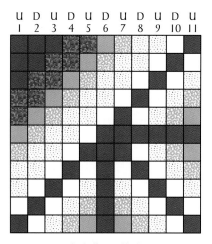

Block #1 – Alfredo
Make 4.
Strip sets on page 88.

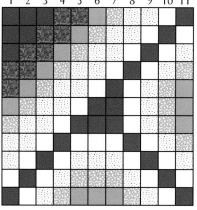

Block #2 – Fettuccine
Make 8.
Strip sets on page 93.

Block #3 – Rebecca
Make 4.
Strip sets on page 99.

BLOCK DESIGN	ALFREDO	FETTUCCINE	REBECCA
Strip Size	2" x 11"	2" x 20"	2" x 11"
NO. OF STRIPS			
■ Dark Dark	32	24	37
▨ Light Dark	9	9	19
▢ Dark Medium	10	12	15
▨ Light Medium	15	17	18
▢ Dark Light	29	31	14
□ Light Light	26	28	18
FROM THE ASSEMBLED STRIP SETS, CUT SEGMENTS AS FOLLOWS:			
Width	2"	2"	2"
No. of Segments	4	8	4

MATERIALS: 44"-WIDE FABRIC

- ⅓ yd. for inner border
- ¾ yd. for outer border
- 4½ yds. for backing
- ⅝ yd. for binding
- 80" x 80" piece of batting

Block Construction

Refer to "Strip Piecing Your Way to a Watercolor Quilt" on pages 17–22 for information on cutting and assembling strip sets and blocks, and to the "Block Gallery" on pages 88–104 for illustrations of the strip sets required.

Crosscut strip sets as directed above and assemble the blocks shown at left.

Quilt Top Assembly

1. Arrange the blocks in 4 rows of 4 blocks each as shown in the quilt plan below, alternating and rotating the blocks as necessary. Sew the blocks together as directed in "Assembling the Quilt Top," page 85.

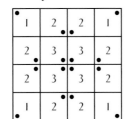

Dots on the quilt plan indicate the upper left corner of the design block.

2. From the inner border fabric, cut 6 strips, each 1½" x 42". From the outer border fabric, cut 6 strips, each 3¼" x 42". Sew the inner and outer border strips together in pairs. Cut 2 pairs of strips in half crosswise. Sew 1 piece to each of the 4 remaining strips, using a diagonal seam as shown on page 85.

3. Measure the quilt top for borders as described in "Borders with Mitered Corners" on page 86. Trim the borders to fit and sew to the quilt top; miter the corners.

4. Layer the quilt top with backing and batting; baste. Quilt as desired.

5. From the binding fabric, cut 7 strips, each 2½" x 42". Join the strips with a diagonal seam to make one piece of binding that is long enough for the quilt. Bind the edges.

HOW DOES MY GARDEN GROW?

by Deanna Spingola, 1995, Woodridge, Illinois. Most gardens begin with seeds or small plants. This one, with a large fan-centered flower, began with a wonderful variety of colorful floral fabrics. Quilted by Dee Pitthan.

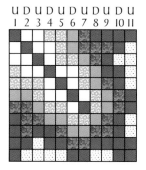

U D U D U D U D U D U
1 2 3 4 5 6 7 8 9 10 11

Block #4 – Rebecca B
Make 4.
Strip sets on page 99.

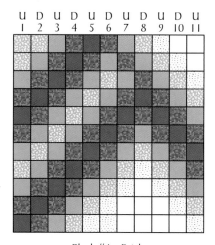

U D U D U D U D U D U
1 2 3 4 5 6 7 8 9 10 11

Block #5 – Rebecca C
Make 8.
Strip sets on page 99.

FINISHED QUILT SIZE: 88" x 88"   ✥   BLOCK SIZES: 16½", 11" x 16", 11"
SKILL LEVEL: Intermediate

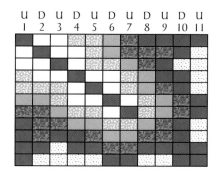

U D U D U D U D U D U
1 2 3 4 5 6 7 8 9 10 11

Block #3 – Rebecca A
Make 8.
Strip sets on page 99.

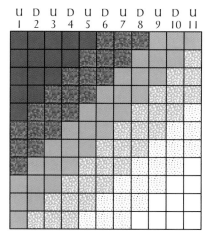

U D U D U D U D U D U
1 2 3 4 5 6 7 8 9 10 11

Block #1 – Petals
Make 8.
Strip sets on page 98.

U D U D U D U D U D U
1 2 3 4 5 6 7 8 9 10 11

Block #2 – Trucioli
Make 8.
Strip sets on page 103.

Block Design	Petals	Trucioli	Rebecca A & B	Rebecca C
Strip Size	2" x 20"	2" x 20"	1½" x 26"	2" x 16"
No. of Strips				
Dark Dark	16	15	37	37
Light Dark	32	21	19	19
Dark Medium	30	30	15	15
Light Medium	21	27	18	18
Dark Light	11	18	14	14
Light Light	11	10	18	18
From the assembled strip sets, cut segments as follows:				
Width	2"	2"	1½"	1½"
No. of Segments	8	8	4	8
Width	—	—	2"	—
No. of Segments	—	—	8	—

MATERIALS: 44"-WIDE FABRIC

- ¾ yd. for binding
- 8 yds. for backing
- 96" x 96" piece of batting

Block Construction

Refer to "Strip Piecing Your Way to a Watercolor Quilt" on pages 17–22 for information on cutting and assembling strip sets and blocks, and to the "Block Gallery" on pages 88–104 for illustrations of the strip sets required.

Crosscut strip sets as directed above and assemble the blocks shown at left. Use the same fabrics for the strip sets in the Rebecca A, B, and C blocks.

Quilt Top Assembly

1. Arrange the blocks in 6 rows of 6 blocks each as shown in the quilt plan below, alternating and rotating the blocks as necessary. Sew the blocks together as directed in "Assembling the Quilt Top" on page 85.

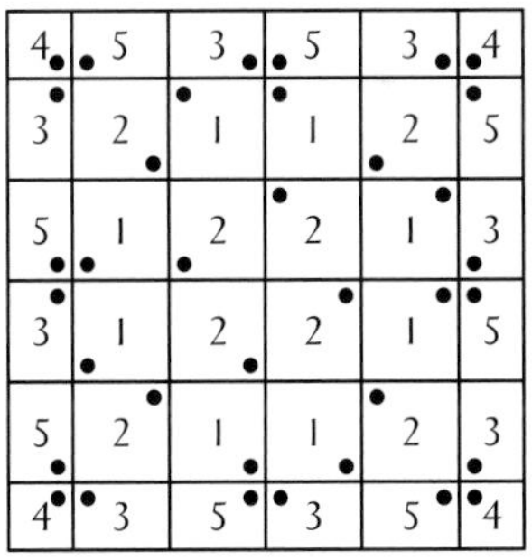

4	5	3	5	3	4
3	2	1	1	2	5
5	1	2	2	1	3
3	1	2	2	1	5
5	2	1	1	2	3
4	3	5	3	5	4

Dots on the quilt plan indicate the upper left corner of the design block.

2. Layer the quilt top with backing and batting; baste. Quilt as desired.
3. From the binding fabric, cut 9 strips, each 2½" x 42". Join the strips with a diagonal seam to make one piece of binding that is long enough for the quilt. Bind the edges.

SPRINGBROOK GARDEN

by Dee Pitthan, 1996, Rockford, Illinois. This quilt is a great example of the manipulation of predominantly cool colors, accentuated by the dark-value outer border and bright turquoise inner border.

FINISHED QUILT SIZE: 76" x 76"   ❖   BLOCK SIZE: 16½"   ❖   SKILL LEVEL: Intermediate

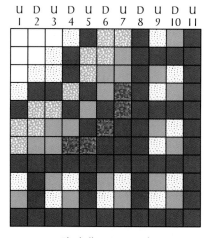

Block #1 – Memorial
Make 4.
Strip sets on page 95.

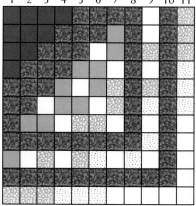

Block #2 – Maggio
Make 4.
Strip sets on page 95.

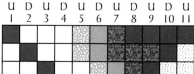

Block #3 – Rebecca
Make 8.
Strip sets on page 99.

BLOCK DESIGN	MEMORIAL	MAGGIO	REBECCA
Strip Size	2" x 11"	2" x 11"	2" x 20"
NO. OF STRIPS			
■ Dark Dark	61	10	37
▨ Light Dark	5	52	19
▦ Dark Medium	21	12	15
▨ Light Medium	11	14	18
⬚ Dark Light	17	10	14
☐ Light Light	6	23	18
FROM THE ASSEMBLED STRIP SETS, CUT SEGMENTS AS FOLLOWS:			
Width	2"	2"	2"
No. of Segments	4	4	8

MATERIALS: 44"-WIDE FABRIC

- ⅜ yd. for inner border
- 1⅛ yds. for outer border
- ⅝ yd. for binding
- 4⅝ yds. for backing
- 82" x 82" piece of batting

Block Construction

Refer to "Strip Piecing Your Way to a Watercolor Quilt" on pages 17–22 for information on cutting and assembling strip sets and blocks, and to the "Block Gallery" on pages 88–104 for illustrations of the strip sets required.

Crosscut strip sets as directed above and assemble the blocks shown at left.

Quilt Top Assembly

1. Arrange the blocks in 4 rows of 4 blocks each as shown in the quilt plan below, alternating and rotating the blocks as necessary. Sew the blocks together as directed in "Assembling the Quilt Top," page 85.

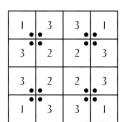

Dots on the quilt plan indicate the upper left corner of the design block.

2. From the inner border fabric, cut 8 strips, each 1¼" x 42". From the outer border fabric, cut 8 strips, each 4½" x 42". Sew the inner and outer border strips together; sew pairs of strips together with a diagonal seam as shown on page 85.

3. Measure the quilt top for borders as described in "Borders with Mitered Corners" on page 86. Trim the borders to fit and sew to the quilt top; miter the corners.

4. Layer the quilt top with backing and batting; baste. Quilt as desired.

5. From the binding fabric, cut 8 strips, each 2½" x 42". Join the strips with a diagonal seam to make one piece of binding that is long enough for the quilt. Bind the edges.

STAINED-GLASS GARDEN

by Linda Garzynski, 1996, Downers Grove, Illinois. This quilt reminds Linda of her Uncle Lee's garden in Santa Rosa, California, where she used to visit as a child. His wonderful flowers created a myriad of color similar to the color peeking out from behind the "gingerbread" in this quilt.

FINISHED QUILT SIZE: 73" x 73"   ◈   BLOCK SIZE: 16½"   ◈   SKILL LEVEL: Intermediate

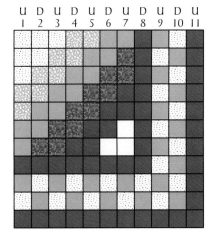

Block #1 – Eleven Square One
Make 4.
Strip sets on page 92.

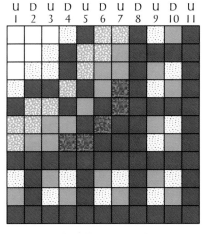

Block #2 – Memorial
Make 12.
Strip sets on page 95.

BLOCK DESIGN	ELEVEN SQUARE ONE	MEMORIAL
Strip Size	2" x 11"	2" x 27"

NO. OF STRIPS

■	Dark Dark	43	61
▨	Light Dark	11	5
▦	Dark Medium	31	21
▨	Light Medium	9	11
▨	Dark Light	24	17
□	Light Light	3	6

FROM THE ASSEMBLED STRIP SETS, CUT SEGMENTS AS FOLLOWS:

Width	2"	2"
No. of Segments	4	12

MATERIALS: 44"-WIDE FABRIC

- ½ yd. for inner border
- ¾ yd. for outer border
- ⅝ yd. for binding
- 4½ yds. for backing
- 79" x 79" piece of batting

Block Construction

Refer to "Strip Piecing Your Way to a Watercolor Quilt" on pages 17–22 for information on cutting and assembling strip sets and blocks, and to the "Block Gallery" on pages 88–104 for illustrations of the strip sets required.

Crosscut strip sets as directed above and assemble the blocks shown at left.

Quilt Top Assembly

1. Arrange the blocks in 4 rows of 4 blocks each as shown in the quilt plan below, alternating and rotating the blocks as necessary. Sew the blocks together as directed in "Assembling the Quilt Top," page 85.

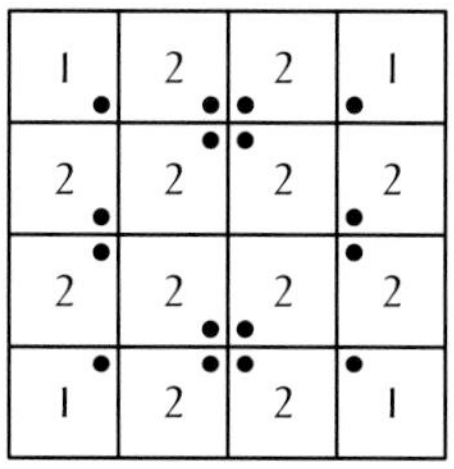

1	2	2	1
2	2	2	2
2	2	2	2
1	2	2	1

Dots on the quilt plan indicate the upper left corner of the design block.

2. From the inner border fabric, cut 8 strips, each 1½" x 42". From the outer border fabric, cut 8 strips, each 2¾" x 42". Sew the inner and outer border strips together; sew pairs of strips together with a diagonal seam as shown on page 85.

3. Measure the quilt top for borders as described in "Borders with Mitered Corners" on page 86. Trim the borders to fit and sew to the quilt top; miter the corners.

4. Layer the quilt top with backing and batting; baste. Quilt as desired.

5. From the binding fabric, cut 7 strips, each 2½" x 42". Join the strips with a diagonal seam to make one piece of binding that is long enough for the quilt. Bind the edges.

GLORIOSO

by Dorothy Larsen, 1996, Naperville, Illinois. A centered diamond, bordered with a checkered square, shows little windows of light and creates the drama in this unique and beautiful quilt.

FINISHED QUILT SIZE: 80" x 80" ◈ BLOCK SIZE: 16½" ◈ SKILL LEVEL: Intermediate

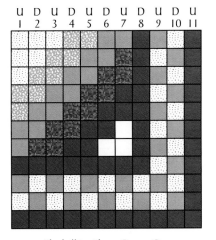

Block #1 – Eleven Square One
Make 4.
Strip sets on page 92.

Block #2 – Memorial
Make 4.
Strip sets on page 95.

Block #3 – Rebecca
Make 8.
Strip sets on page 99.

66

Block Design	Eleven Square One	Memorial	Rebecca
Strip Size	2" x 11"	2" x 11"	2" x 20"
No. of Strips			
■ Dark Dark	43	61	37
▦ Light Dark	11	5	19
▨ Dark Medium	31	21	15
▧ Light Medium	9	11	18
▫ Dark Light	24	17	14
□ Light Light	3	6	18
From the assembled strip sets, cut segments as follows:			
Width	2"	2"	2"
No. of Segments	4	4	8

MATERIALS: 44"-WIDE FABRIC

- ⅝ yd. for inner border
- 1⅜ yds. for outer border
- ⅝ yd. for binding
- 5 yds. for backing
- 88" x 88" piece of batting

Block Construction

Refer to "Strip Piecing Your Way to a Watercolor Quilt" on pages 17–22 for information on cutting and assembling strip sets and blocks, and to the "Block Gallery" on pages 88–104 for illustrations of the strip sets required.

Crosscut strip sets as directed above and assemble the blocks shown at left.

Quilt Top Assembly

1. Arrange the blocks in 4 rows of 4 blocks each as shown in the quilt plan below, alternating and rotating the blocks as necessary. Sew the blocks together as directed in "Assembling the Quilt Top" on page 85.

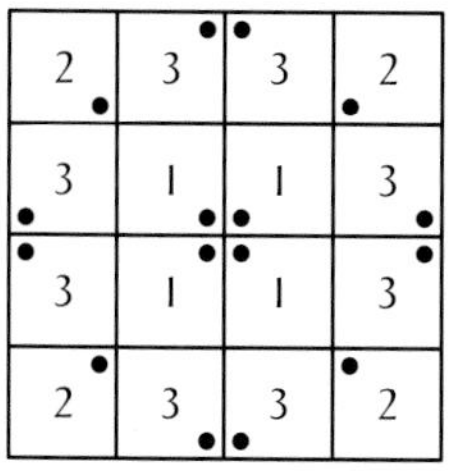

2	3	3	2
3	1	1	3
3	1	1	3
2	3	3	2

Dots on the quilt plan indicate the
upper left corner of the design block.

2. From the inner border fabric, cut 8 strips, each 2½" x 42". From the outer border fabric, cut 8 strips, each 5¼" x 42". Sew the inner and outer border strips together; sew pairs of strips together with a diagonal seam as shown on page 85.
3. Measure the quilt top for borders as described in "Borders with Mitered Corners" on page 86. Trim the borders to fit and sew to the quilt top; miter the corners.
4. Layer the quilt top with backing and batting; baste. Quilt as desired.
5. From the binding fabric, cut 8 strips, each 2½" x 42". Join the strips with a diagonal seam to make one piece of binding that is long enough for the quilt. Bind the edges.

CENTRIFUGAL COLORS

by Deanna Spingola, 1996, Woodridge, Illinois. The quilting accentuates the circular motion and energy created by the combination of warm colors and strategic placement of values. Quilted by Quilt Acclaim.

FINISHED QUILT SIZE: 75½" x 75½"   ◈   BLOCK SIZE: 16½"   ◈   SKILL LEVEL: INTERMEDIATE

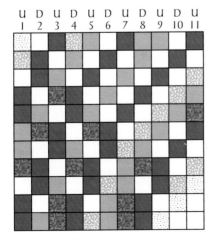

U D U D U D U D U D U
1 2 3 4 5 6 7 8 9 10 11

Block #1 – Circle
Make 12.
Strip sets on page 89.

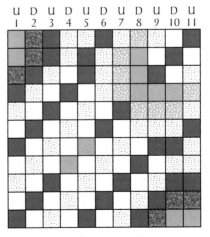

U D U D U D U D U D U
1 2 3 4 5 6 7 8 9 10 11

Block #2 – Corner Block
Make 4.
Strip sets on page 90.

BLOCK DESIGN		CIRCLE	CORNER BLOCK
Strip Size		2"x 27"	2" x 11"
NO. OF STRIPS			
■	Dark Dark	33	30
▨	Light Dark	11	6
▨	Dark Medium	23	11
▨	Light Medium	11	8
▨	Dark Light	4	32
□	Light Light	39	34

FROM THE ASSEMBLED STRIP SETS,
CUT SEGMENTS AS FOLLOWS:

Width	2"	2"
No. of Segments	12	4

MATERIALS: 44"-WIDE FABRIC

- ½ yd. for inner border
- 1 yd. for outer border
- ¾ yd. for binding
- 4½ yds. for backing
- 80" x 80" piece of batting

Block Construction

Refer to "Strip Piecing Your Way to a Watercolor Quilt" on pages 17–22 for information on cutting and assembling strip sets and blocks, and to the "Block Gallery" on pages 88–104 for illustrations of the strip sets required.

Crosscut strip sets as directed above and assemble the blocks shown at left.

Quilt Top Assembly

1. Arrange the blocks in 4 rows of 4 blocks each as shown in the quilt plan below, alternating and rotating the blocks as necessary. Sew the blocks together as directed in "Assembling the Quilt Top" on page 85.

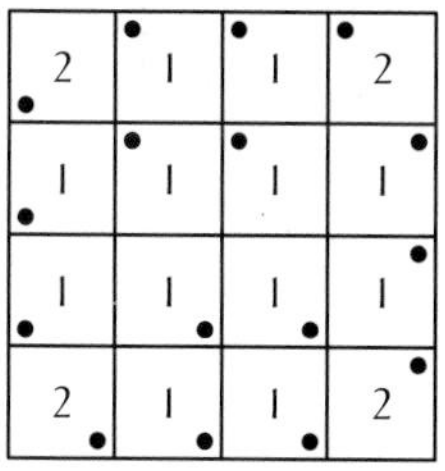

Dots on the quilt plan indicate the
upper left corner of the design block.

2. From the inner border fabric, cut 8 strips, each 1¾" x 42". From the outer border fabric, cut 8 strips, each 3¾" x 42". Sew the inner and outer border strips together, then sew pairs of strip units together with a diagonal seam as shown on page 85.

3. Measure the quilt top for borders as described in "Borders with Mitered Corners" on page 86. Trim the borders to fit and sew to the quilt top; miter the corners.

4. Layer the quilt top with backing and batting; baste. Quilt as desired.

5. From the binding fabric, cut 8 strips, each 2½" x 42". Join the strips with a diagonal seam to make one piece of binding that is long enough for the quilt. Bind the edges.

CHICAGO: HOPE TO QUILT

by Rae A. Kittleson, 1996, Anoka, Minnesota. The light-value, propeller-style center appears to be surrounded by a round garland of dark flowers that intertwine, creating more dimension and interesting lines.

FINISHED QUILT SIZE: 61½" x 61½" ✦ BLOCK SIZES: 16½", 11" x 16½", 11" ✦ SKILL LEVEL: Intermediate

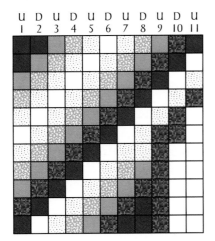

Block # 1 – Montie Two
Make 4.
Strip sets on page 96.

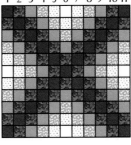

Block #2 – Diamonds
Make 4.
Strip sets on page 91.

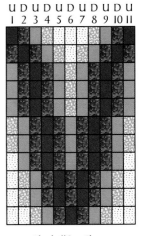

Block #3 – Clover
Make 8.
Strip sets on page 90.

BLOCK DESIGN	MONTIE TWO	DIAMONDS	CLOVER
Strip Size	2" x 11"	1½" x 9"	2" x 16"

NO. OF STRIPS

		MONTIE TWO	DIAMONDS	CLOVER
■	Dark Dark	17	21	21
▦	Light Dark	22	36	38
▨	Dark Medium	16	28	31
▧	Light Medium	16	20	17
▫	Dark Light	22	12	14
□	Light Light	28	4	0

FROM THE ASSEMBLED STRIP SETS, CUT SEGMENTS AS FOLLOWS:

	MONTIE TWO	DIAMONDS	CLOVER
Width	2"	1½"	1½"
No. of Segments	4	4	8

MATERIALS: 44"-WIDE FABRIC

- ¾ yd. for border
- ½ yd. for binding
- 3¾ yds. for backing
- 68" x 68" piece of batting

Block Construction

Refer to "Strip Piecing Your Way to a Watercolor Quilt" on pages 17–22 for information on cutting and assembling strip sets and blocks, and to the "Block Gallery" on pages 88–104 for illustrations of the strip sets required.

Crosscut strip sets as directed above and assemble the blocks shown at left.

Quilt Top Assembly

1. Arrange the blocks in 4 rows of 4 blocks each as shown in the quilt plan below, alternating and rotating the blocks as necessary. Sew the blocks together as directed in "Assembling the Quilt Top" on page 85.

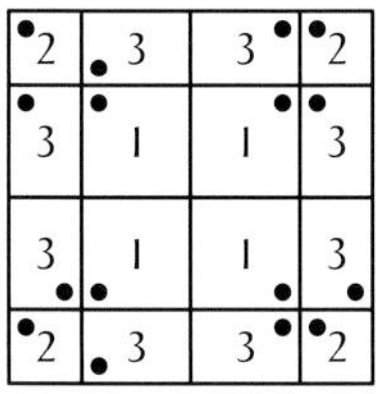

•2	•3	3•	•2
•3	•1	1•	3•
3	1	1	3
•2	•3	3•	•2

Dots on the quilt plan indicate the upper left corner of the design block.

2. From the border fabric, cut 6 strips, each 3½" x 42". Cut 2 strips in half crosswise and sew 1 piece to each of the 4 remaining strips, using a diagonal seam as shown on page 85.

3. Measure the quilt top for borders as described in "Borders with Straight-Cut Corners" on page 87. Trim 2 strips to fit the side edges and sew to opposite sides of the quilt top. Trim the 2 remaining strips to fit the top and bottom edges and sew to the quilt top.

4. Layer the quilt top with backing and batting; baste. Quilt as desired.

5. From the binding fabric, cut 6 strips, each 2½" x 42". Join the strips with a diagonal seam to make one piece of binding that is long enough for the quilt. Bind the edges.

AURORA BOREALIS

by Barbara Boyd, 1996, Eagan, Minnesota. This design reminds Barbara of the Northern Lights often seen in Minnesota. It is machine and hand quilted with metallic thread. The rich hand-quilted purple border accentuates the great purple fabrics used in the body of the quilt.

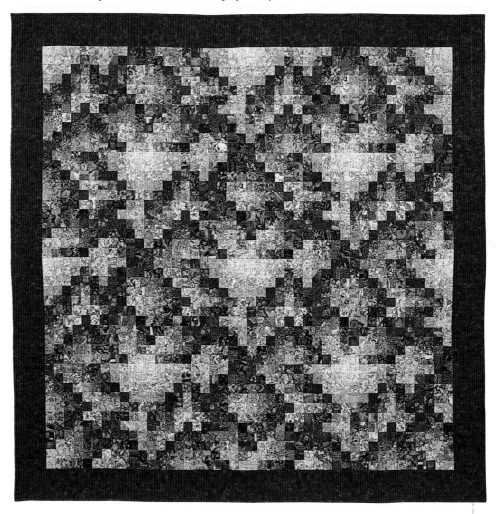

FINISHED QUILT SIZE: 75½" x 75½" ❖ BLOCK SIZE: 16½" ❖ SKILL LEVEL: Beginner

Peaks
Make 16.
Strip sets on page 97.

BLOCK DESIGN	PEAKS
Strip Size	2" x 36"

NO. OF STRIPS

■	Dark Dark	25
▨	Light Dark	22
▨	Dark Medium	21
▨	Light Medium	24
▨	Dark Light	26
□	Light Light	3

FROM THE ASSEMBLED STRIP SETS,
CUT SEGMENTS AS FOLLOWS:

Width	2"
No. of Segments	16

MATERIALS: 44"-WIDE FABRIC

- 1¼ yds. for border
- ⅔ yd. for binding
- 5 yds. for backing
- 81" x 81" piece of batting

Block Construction

Refer to "Strip Piecing Your Way to a Watercolor Quilt" on pages 17–22 for information on cutting and assembling strip sets and blocks, and to the "Block Gallery" on pages 88–104 for illustrations of the strip sets required.

Crosscut strip sets as directed above and assemble the blocks shown at left.

Quilt Top Assembly

1. Arrange the blocks in 4 rows of 4 blocks each as shown in the quilt plan below, rotating the blocks as necessary. Sew the blocks together as directed in "Assembling the Quilt Top," page 85.

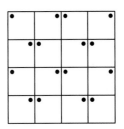

Dots on the quilt plan indicate the
upper left corner of the design block.

2. From the border fabric, cut 8 strips, each 5" x 42". Sew pairs of border strips together with a diagonal seam as shown on page 85.
3. Measure the quilt top for borders as described in "Borders with Mitered Corners" on page 86. Trim the borders to fit and sew to the quilt top; miter the corners.
4. Layer the quilt top with backing and batting; baste. Quilt as desired.
5. From the binding fabric, cut 8 strips, each 2½" x 42". Join the strips with a diagonal seam to make one piece of binding that is long enough for the quilt. Bind the edges.

WANDERING THROUGH THE FENCE

by Wanda S. Hanson, 1996, Sandwich, Illinois. Wanda cut ovals of various shades of subtle hand-dyed fabrics to make the unique raw-edge, machine-appliquéd flowers that adorn this wonderful, ethereal, misty garden.

FINISHED QUILT SIZE: 44" x 62" ❖ BLOCK SIZE: 18" ❖ SKILL LEVEL: Intermediate

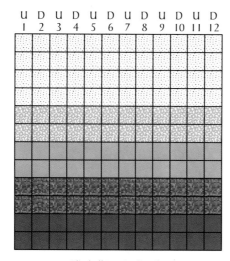

Block #1 – Garden Sky
Make 4.
Strip sets on page 93.

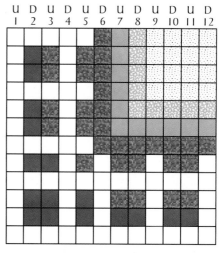

Block #2 – Picket Fence
Make 2.
Strip sets on page 98.

Block Design	Garden Sky	Picket Fence
Strip Size	2" x 11"	2" x 6"

NO. OF STRIPS		
▪ Dark Dark	24	16
▪ Light Dark	24	30
▪ Dark Medium	24	11
▪ Light Medium	24	9
▪ Dark Light	48	16
□ Light Light	0	62

FROM THE ASSEMBLED STRIP SETS,

CUT SEGMENTS AS FOLLOWS:

Width	2"	2"
No. of Segments	4	2

MATERIALS: 44"-WIDE FABRIC

- Assorted scraps of green and pastel-colored solids for appliqué
- ¾ yd. for border
- ⅝ yd. for binding
- 3½ yds. for backing
- 50" x 66" piece of batting

Block Construction

Refer to "Strip Piecing Your Way to a Watercolor Quilt" on pages 17–22 for information on cutting and assembling strip sets and blocks, and to the "Block Gallery" on pages 88–104 for illustrations of the strip sets required.

Crosscut strip sets as directed above and assemble the blocks shown at left.

Quilt Top Assembly

1. Arrange the blocks in 2 rows of 3 blocks each as shown in the quilt plan below, alternating and rotating the blocks as necessary. Sew the blocks together as directed in "Assembling the Quilt Top" on page 85.

Dots on the quilt plan indicate the upper left corner of the design block.

2. From the border fabric, cut 6 strips, each 4¼" x 42". Measure the quilt top for borders as described in "Borders with Straight-Cut Corners" on page 87. Trim 2 strips to fit the side edges and sew to opposite sides of the quilt top. Sew the 4 remaining strips together in pairs, using a diagonal seam as shown on page 85. Trim the strips to fit and sew to the top and bottom edges.

3. Cut appliqué pieces, using the template patterns on page 107. Cut stems and leaves from appropriately colored fabrics and pin to the quilt top. Refer to the quilt photo at left for placement. Using raw-edge appliqué techniques as described on page 84, stitch the stems and leaves to the quilt top. Try using rayon thread in a shade that is slightly darker than the appliqués for a decorative effect. Cut flowers from the pastel fabrics and pin them to the quilt top; machine stitch in place.

4. Layer the quilt top with backing and batting; baste. Quilt as desired. Quilt around, but not on, the flowers, stems, and leaves.

5. From the binding fabric, cut 6 strips, each 3½" x 42". Join the strips with a diagonal seam to make one piece of binding that is long enough for the quilt. Bind the edges, using a ½"-wide seam allowance.

RAINBOW WEAVE TWELVE

by Deanna Spingola, 1996, Woodridge, Illinois. Two block patterns work well together to create this optical treat. Colors and values weave over and under in the Twelve Weave block, while the alternate block adds more dimension.

FINISHED QUILT SIZE: 59½" x 59½" ✦ BLOCK SIZE: 18" ✦ SKILL LEVEL: Advanced

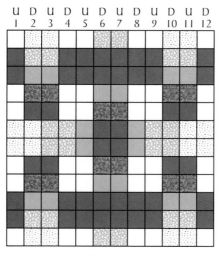

Block #1 – Twelve Weave
Make 5.
Strip sets on page 103.

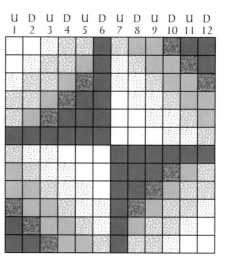

Block #2 – Boomerang Two
Make 4.
Strip sets on page 89.

Block Design	Twelve Weave	Boomerang Two
Strip Size	2" x 13"	2" x 11"

NO. OF STRIPS

	Twelve Weave	Boomerang Two
■ Dark Dark	44	34
▨ Light Dark	12	12
▤ Dark Medium	16	26
▦ Light Medium	20	30
▥ Dark Light	16	24
□ Light Light	36	18

FROM THE ASSEMBLED STRIP SETS, CUT SEGMENTS AS FOLLOWS:

	Twelve Weave	Boomerang Two
Width	2"	2"
No. of Segments	5	4

MATERIALS: 44"-WIDE FABRIC

- ⅝ yd. for border
- ¾ yd. for binding
- 3¾ yds. for backing
- 66" x 66" piece of batting

Block Construction

❧ Note ❧

The weave blocks require special attention to ensure that the visual illusion of the over-and-under weave is carried through the block. The following steps will help you achieve this goal.

1. Make sure 1½" of each fabric is showing for a clear view of the block you are constructing.
2. Check the values to make sure the dark-dark fabrics are evenly dark on both sides of the lighter strips. Use a reducing tool or the Ruby Beholder to check the values.
3. Stand back from the strips after you lay them out and make sure you can see the weave.

Refer to "Strip Piecing Your Way to a Watercolor Quilt" on pages 17–22 for information on cutting and assembling strip sets and blocks, and to the "Block Gallery" on pages 88–104 for illustrations of the strip sets required.

Crosscut strip sets as directed above and assemble the blocks shown at left.

Quilt Top Assembly

1. Arrange the blocks in 3 rows of 3 blocks each as shown in the quilt plan below, alternating and rotating the blocks as necessary. Sew the blocks together as directed in "Assembling the Quilt Top" on page 85.

Dots on the quilt plan indicate the
upper left corner of the design block.

2. From the border fabric, cut 6 strips of fabric, each 3" x 42". Cut 2 strips in half crosswise and sew 1 piece to each of the 4 remaining strips, using a diagonal seam as shown on page 85.
3. Measure the quilt top for borders as described in "Borders with Mitered Corners" on page 86. Trim the borders to fit and sew to the quilt top; miter the corners.
4. Layer the quilt top with backing and batting; baste. Quilt as desired.
5. From the binding fabric, cut 6 strips, each 3½" x 42". Join the strips with a diagonal seam to make one piece of binding that is long enough to bind the quilt. Bind the edges, using a ½"-wide seam allowance.

ℛAINBOW
WEAVE REVIEW

by Deanna Spingola, 1996, Woodridge, Illinois. Light, medium, and dark values weave over and under in this colorful quilt, reminiscent of a Celtic cross. The intersections are defined by light areas, and "gingerbread" highlights the corners.

FINISHED QUILT SIZE: 59" x 59" ◈ BLOCK SIZE: 18" ◈ SKILL LEVEL: **Advanced**

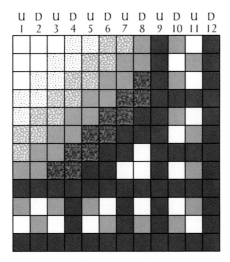

Block #1 – Twelve Square One
Make 4.
Strip sets on page 103.

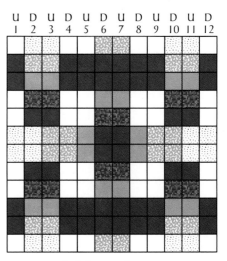

Block #2 – Twelve Weave
Make 5.
Strip sets on page 103.

BLOCK DESIGN	TWELVE SQUARE ONE	TWELVE WEAVE
Strip Size	2" x 11"	2" x 14"

NO. OF STRIPS

	TWELVE SQUARE ONE	TWELVE WEAVE
■ Dark Dark	59	44
▨ Light Dark	11	12
▦ Dark Medium	29	16
▨ Light Medium	13	20
▫ Dark Light	23	16
☐ Light Light	9	36

FROM THE ASSEMBLED STRIP SETS, CUT SEGMENTS AS FOLLOWS:

	TWELVE SQUARE ONE	TWELVE WEAVE
Width	2"	2"
No. of Segments	4	5

MATERIALS: 44"-WIDE FABRIC

- ⅝ yd. for border
- ¾ yd. for binding
- 3¾ yds. for backing
- 65" x 65" piece of batting

Block Construction

❧ Note ☙
The weave blocks require special attention to ensure that the visual illusion of the over-and-under weave is carried through the block. The following steps will help you achieve this goal.

1. Make sure 1½" of each fabric is showing for a clear view of the block you are constructing.
2. Check the values to make sure the dark-dark fabrics are evenly dark on both sides of the lighter strips. Use a reducing tool or the Ruby Beholder to check the values.
3. Stand back from the strips after you lay them out and make sure you can see the weave.

Refer to "Strip Piecing Your Way to a Watercolor Quilt" on pages 17–22 for information on cutting and assembling strip sets and blocks, and to the "Block Gallery" on pages 88–104 for illustrations of the strip sets required.

Crosscut strip sets as directed above and assemble the blocks shown at left.

Quilt Top Assembly

1. Arrange the blocks in 3 rows of 3 blocks each as shown in the quilt plan below, alternating and rotating the blocks as necessary. Sew the blocks together as directed in "Assembling the Quilt Top" on page 85.

Dots on the quilt plan indicate the upper left corner of the design block.

2. From the border fabric, cut 6 strips, each 2¾" x 42". Cut 2 strips in half crosswise and sew 1 piece to each of the 4 remaining strips, using a diagonal seam as shown on page 85.
3. Measure the quilt top for borders as described in "Borders with Mitered Corners" on page 86. Trim the borders to fit and sew to the quilt top; miter the corners.
4. Layer the quilt top with backing and batting; baste. Quilt as desired.
5. From the binding fabric, cut 6 strips, each 3½" x 42". Join the strips with a diagonal seam to make one piece of binding that is long enough to bind the quilt. Bind the edges, using a ½"-wide seam allowance.

SHADOW ROMANCE

by Denise Griffin, 1996, Downers Grove, Illinois. Beautiful fans of color cascade across the surface of this quilt, destined for a lovely little girl to snuggle under and dream sweet dreams.

FINISHED QUILT SIZE: 76½" x 109½" ❖ BLOCK SIZE: 16½" ❖ SKILL LEVEL: Intermediate

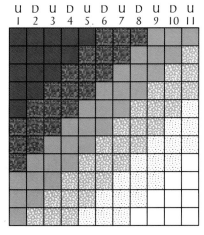

Trucioli
Make 24.
Strip sets on page 103.

❧ *Note* ❧
Because the quilt requires 24 blocks,
1 group of strip sets is insufficient.
Make 1 set with 40"-wide strips
and another set with 11"-wide
strips. Both strip sets should be
made with the same fabric.

BLOCK	TRUCIOLI
Strip Size	2" x 40" and 2" x 11"

NO. OF STRIPS

■	Dark Dark	15
▨	Light Dark	21
▦	Dark Medium	30
▤	Light Medium	27
⬚	Dark Light	18
☐	Light Light	10

FROM THE ASSEMBLED STRIP SETS,

CUT SEGMENTS AS FOLLOWS:

Width	2"
No. of Segments	24

MATERIALS: 44"-WIDE FABRIC

- 1¾ yds. for border
- ¾ yd. for binding
- 6½ yds. for backing
- 83" x 116" piece of batting

Block Construction

Refer to "Strip Piecing Your Way to a Watercolor Quilt" on pages 17–22 for information on cutting and assembling strip sets and blocks, and to the "Block Gallery" on pages 88–104 for illustrations of the strip sets required.

Crosscut strip sets as directed above and assemble the blocks shown at left.

Quilt Top Assembly

1. Arrange the blocks in 6 rows of 4 blocks each as shown in the quilt plan at right, rotating the blocks as necessary. Sew them together as directed in "Assembling the Quilt Top" on page 85.

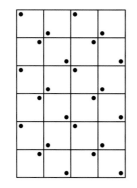

Dots on the quilt plan indicate the upper left corner of the design block.

꒰ Note ꒱
The maker of this quilt chose six different fabrics for the border.

2. From the border fabric, cut 10 strips, each 5½" x 42". For each side border, sew 3 strips together, using a diagonal seam as shown on page 85, to make one long strip. For the top and bottom borders, join 2 strips with a diagonal seam.

3. Measure the quilt top for borders as described in "Borders with Mitered Corners" on page 86. Trim the borders to fit and sew to the quilt top; miter the corners.

4. Layer the quilt top with backing and batting; baste. Quilt as desired.

5. From the binding fabric, cut 10 strips, each 2½" x 42". Join the strips with a diagonal seam to make one piece of binding that is long enough for the quilt. Bind the edges.

by Deanna Spingola, 1996, Woodridge, Illinois. This batik panel quilt was inspired by "Going Home," a watercolor quilt created by Drew Donnelly Benage, which appeared in Watercolor Impressions.

FINISHED QUILT SIZE: 40" x 40" ◈ BLOCK SIZE: 8" ◈ SKILL LEVEL: Intermediate

U D U D U D U D
1 2 3 4 5 6 7 8

U D U D U D U D
1 2 3 4 5 6 7 8

Block #1 – Mediator
Make 8.
Strip sets on page 95.

Block #2 – Corner Lot
Make 4.
Strip sets on page 90.

Block Design		Mediator	Corner Lot
	Strip Size	1½" x 15"	1½" x 8"
	No. of Strips		
■	Dark Dark	8	9
▨	Light Dark	10	13
▨	Dark Medium	14	16
▨	Light Medium	14	8
▫	Dark Light	10	13
□	Light Light	8	5

FROM THE ASSEMBLED STRIP SETS,
CUT SEGMENTS AS FOLLOWS:

Width	1½"	1½"
No. of Segments	8	4

MATERIALS: 44"-WIDE FABRIC

- 1 batik panel (choose one that can be trimmed to 16½" x 16½")
- ¼ yd. for inner border
- ½ yd. for outer border
- ½ yd. for binding
- 2½ yds. for backing
- 45" x 45" piece of batting

Block Construction

Refer to "Strip Piecing Your Way to a Watercolor Quilt" on pages 17–22 for information on cutting and assembling strip sets and blocks, and to the "Block Gallery" on pages 88–104 for illustrations of the strip sets required. Use prints that have the same colors as the batik panel.

Crosscut strip sets as directed above and assemble the blocks shown at left.

Quilt Top Assembly

1. Trim the batik panel to 16½" x 16½".
2. Referring to the color photo at left and the quilt plan below, arrange the blocks and batik panel as shown. Sew pairs of Mediator blocks together, then assemble the quilt in rows. Join the rows as directed in "Assembling the Quilt Top" on page 85.

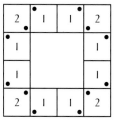

Dots on the quilt plan indicate the
upper left corner of the design block.

3. From the inner border fabric, cut 4 strips, each 1½" x 42". From the outer border fabric, cut 4 strips, each 3" x 42". Sew the inner and outer border strips together.
4. Measure the quilt top for borders as described in "Borders with Mitered Corners" on page 86. Trim the borders to fit and sew them to the quilt top; miter the corners.
5. Layer the quilt top with backing and batting; baste. Quilt as desired.
6. From the binding fabric, cut 4 strips, each 2½" x 42". Join the strips with a diagonal seam to make one piece of binding that is long enough for the quilt. Bind the edges.

Foundation Paper Piecing

"Sunrise Serenade" (page 34) features foundation paper-pieced blocks. In paper piecing, small scraps of fabric are sewn one at a time, in numerical sequence, to a paper foundation. The scraps need to be large enough to cover the numbered area and to allow ¼"-wide seam allowances.

1. For paper-pieced blocks, use a size 90/14 needle and set your machine to about 20 stitches per inch. The larger needle and small stitches make it easier to remove the paper after the blocks are completed.

2. Make copies of the block pattern as directed in the quilt plan. (You may trace it or make photocopies.) If you choose to photocopy, use the original pattern on page 105 and make all the copies on the same machine to prevent distortion. Trim each copied pattern to within ½" of the block pattern.

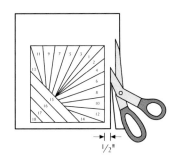

3. Work near a light source so you can readily see through the paper to check fabric placement before sewing. Begin with the fabric scraps cut the size recommended in the materials list. Place fabric #1, right side up, on the wrong side of the pattern. Hold the pattern and fabric up to the light to make certain you have a minimum of ¼"-wide seam allowances on all sides. Pin in place.

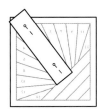

Position fabric #2 on top of fabric #1, right sides together. Turn the pattern to the right side and sew on the stitching line between #1 and #2. Take a few extra stitches beyond the line at the beginning and end. On the outside edge, sew beyond the ¼"-wide seam allowance.

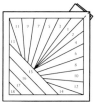

4. Press fabric #2 open. Now position and sew fabric #3. Continue adding fabric, pressing after each addition, until the block is complete. Press, then trim, leaving a ¼"-wide seam allowance all around.

Appliqué

Three styles of appliqué are shown in the quilts: dimensional, traditional, and raw edge. For information on the appliqué techniques used in "The Bouquet" (page 36) and "Be My Valentine" (page 48), refer to *Baltimore Bouquets* by Mimi Dietrich and *The Easy Art of Appliqué* by Mimi Dietrich and Roxi Eppler. They are both good sources of inspiration and instruction.

The raw-edge style of appliqué was designed for people who have an aversion to traditional appliqué, like me. It isn't necessary to turn under the raw edges of the appliqué piece; they will ultimately fray just a little, adding texture and dimension to the quilt.

1. Pin the appliqué pieces in position on the quilt top. Complete all the stems and leaves first, then add the flowers.

2. Use a 7" wooden hoop to stabilize your work area. Place the outer ring of the hoop under the quilt top, then fit the inner ring into the outer ring.

3. Use free-motion stitching to secure the stems and leaves. Sew about ⅛" from the edge. Stitch veins in the leaves and stitch ovals or other shapes in the flowers.

4. With the needle in the down position, remove the hoop and reposition it as necessary without removing the quilt from the machine.

After completing the blocks for your quilt, you are ready to sew them together and add borders. Follow the directions in this section to complete your strip-pieced watercolor quilt top.

1. Arrange the blocks in the order shown in the quilt plan. Rotate them as necessary to the proper position.
2. Determine the best direction to press the vertical seams, then press them to one side. It is best if the seam allowances are pressed in opposite directions from block to block to allow them to nest together, reducing bulk.
3. Sew the blocks together in horizontal rows. Press the seams between the blocks in opposite directions from row to row. Sew the rows together. Trim all stray threads from the back.

Sew blocks together.

4. Make sure opposite edges of the quilt top are the same length. Fold the quilt in half lengthwise to check the sides, then fold it crosswise to check the top and bottom edges. If opposite edges are unequal, press the seams again to remove any tucks, or take slightly deeper seams on several rows. Make adjustments and corrections now; any problems will not magically disappear as you continue.

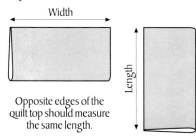

Opposite edges of the quilt top should measure the same length.

Adding Borders

Most of the quilts in this book feature a simple border. Simple works best, unless a pieced border is an integral part of the design, such as in "Sunrise Serenade" (page 34). A border should not be so complex that it detracts from the body of the quilt.

Select the fabric for the border after piecing the quilt top. Determine which values and colors are most prominent in the quilt top, then audition several fabrics that are compatible with or complement those colors or values.

Each quilt plan includes border measurements that correspond to the quilt photo. The yardage is adequate for mitered corners where suggested.

Cutting and Preparing Border Strips

Most of the quilts have borders cut across the grain, from selvage to selvage. A few feature lengthwise strips. When using crosswise strips, piece them by placing two strips, right sides together, at a 90° angle. Position the ¼" line of a ruler exactly at the intersection of the two strips and trim as shown. Pin, then sew the two pieces together, using a ¼"-wide seam allowance. Press the seam open. Use the same technique to join the binding strips.

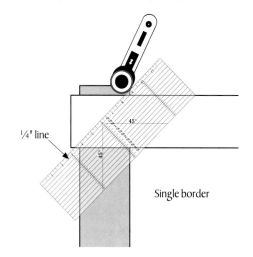

¼" line

Single border

If you are creating a multiple-strip border, sew the strips together to make one wide border unit. To make the border unit longer, place 2 border units, right sides together, at a 90° angle. Match the intersecting seam lines, then cut, stitch, and press the seams open.

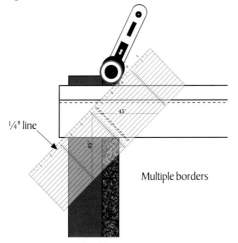

Multiple borders

¼" line

Borders with Mitered Corners

To calculate the strip length for mitered borders, measure the length and width of the quilt through the center. Measure the proposed border width, double that number, and add 4". Add this figure to the width or length of the quilt and cut strips to these measurements.

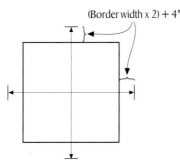

(Border width x 2) + 4"

1. Measure the length of the quilt top through the center. Mark the center of each side of the quilt. Mark the center and edge measurement of the quilt top onto the two border strips. Pin the two side borders to the quilt top, matching the center and edge marks.

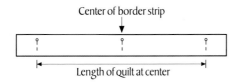

Center of border strip

Length of quilt at center

2. Stitch the border strips to the quilt top, with the border on the bottom and the quilt top wrong side up so you can guide the block seams in the proper direction. Start and stop the stitching ¼" from each edge. Press the seam allowances toward the border.

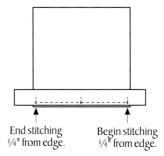

End stitching ¼" from edge.   Begin stitching ¼" from edge.

3. Measure the width of the quilt top through the center. Do not include the side borders. Mark, pin, and stitch the top and bottom border strips to the quilt as you did the side borders. Press the seam allowances toward the borders.

4. To miter the first corner, place the quilt on a flat, hard surface, wrong side up. Overlap the two border strips at a 90° angle. With a ruler and a marking tool, draw a line from the stitching line in the corner of the quilt top to the intersection of the two overlapping border strips as shown. Now, switch the border strips, placing the bottom strip on top. Draw another line in the same manner. Mark the remaining three corners in the same manner.

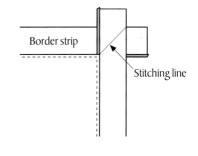

Border strip

Stitching line

5. Fold the quilt diagonally as shown. Aligning the stitching lines, pin the border strips together at the corner. Stitch on the drawn line, beginning at the corner of the quilt top at the end of the stitching line. Trim the seam allowances to ½" and press open. Repeat for remaining corners.

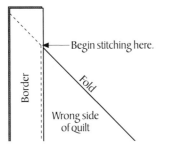

Borders with Straight-Cut Corners

1. Measure the length of the quilt top through the center. Cut two side borders to that length. Fold the two border strips in half, then in quarters. With a pin, mark each division. Repeat with the quilt top. Pin the border strips to the quilt, matching the markings.

2. Stitch the border strips to the quilt top, easing as necessary. Stitch with the quilt top on top so you can guide the quilt-top seams in the proper direction. Press the seam allowances toward the border.

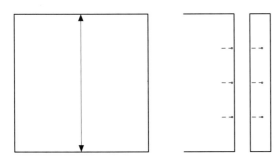

3. Measure the width of the quilt top through the center, including the side borders. Cut the top and bottom border strips to that length. Fold and mark the edge of the quilt and border strips as before. Pin the strips to the quilt, matching the markings.

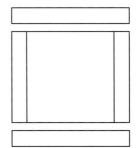

4. Stitch the border strips to the top and bottom of the quilt top, easing as necessary. Press the seam allowances toward the border.

❧ *Note* ❧
If you are adding more than one border with straight-cut corners to your quilt, add each one separately. Do not sew them together before attaching them.

BLOCK GALLERY

Act Four

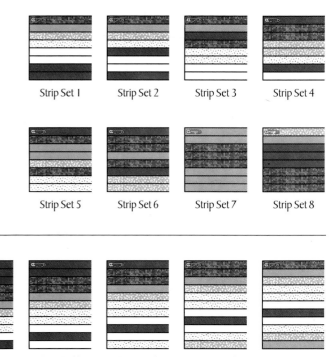

u D u D u D u D
1 2 3 4 5 6 7 8

Strip Set 1   Strip Set 2   Strip Set 3   Strip Set 4

Strip Set 5   Strip Set 6   Strip Set 7   Strip Set 8

Alfredo

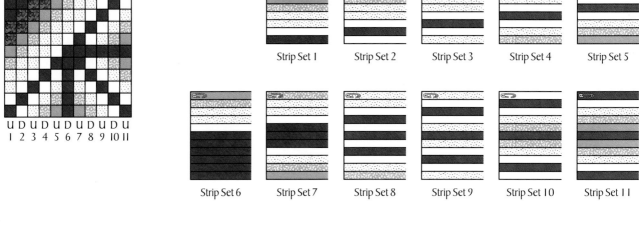

u D u D u D u D u D u
1 2 3 4 5 6 7 8 9 10 11

Strip Set 1   Strip Set 2   Strip Set 3   Strip Set 4   Strip Set 5

Strip Set 6   Strip Set 7   Strip Set 8   Strip Set 9   Strip Set 10   Strip Set 11

Barcelona

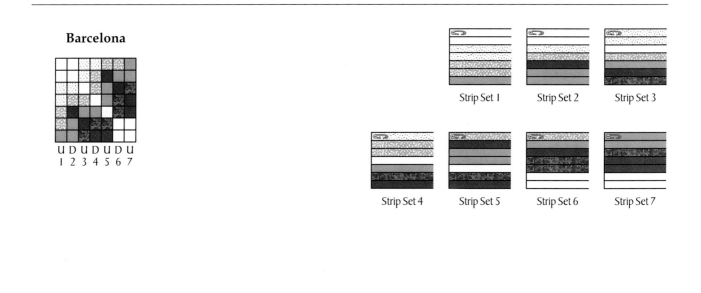

u D u D u D u
1 2 3 4 5 6 7

Strip Set 1   Strip Set 2   Strip Set 3

Strip Set 4   Strip Set 5   Strip Set 6   Strip Set 7

■ Dark Dark   ▦ Light Dark   ▨ Dark Medium   ▨ Light Medium   ▫ Dark Light   □ Light Light

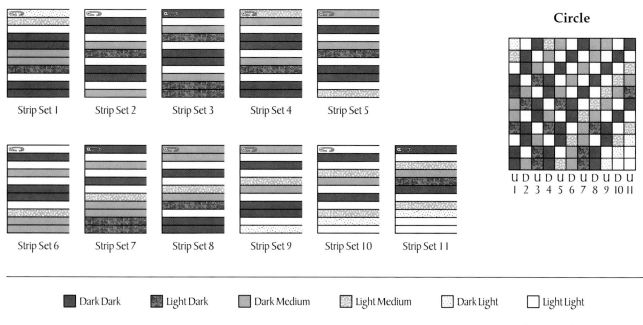

Beguile

U D U D U D U
1 2 3 4 5 6 7

Strip Set 1 **Strip Set 2** **Strip Set 3**

Strip Set 4 **Strip Set 5** **Strip Set 6** **Strip Set 7**

Boomerang Two

U D U D U D U D U D U D
1 2 3 4 5 6 7 8 9 10 11 12

Strip Set 1 **Strip Set 2** **Strip Set 3** **Strip Set 4** **Strip Set 5** **Strip Set 6**

Strip Set 7 **Strip Set 8** **Strip Set 9** **Strip Set 10** **Strip Set 11** **Strip Set 12**

Circle

U D U D U D U D U D U
1 2 3 4 5 6 7 8 9 10 11

Strip Set 1 **Strip Set 2** **Strip Set 3** **Strip Set 4** **Strip Set 5**

Strip Set 6 **Strip Set 7** **Strip Set 8** **Strip Set 9** **Strip Set 10** **Strip Set 11**

■ Dark Dark   ▦ Light Dark   ▨ Dark Medium   ▨ Light Medium   ▫ Dark Light   ▢ Light Light

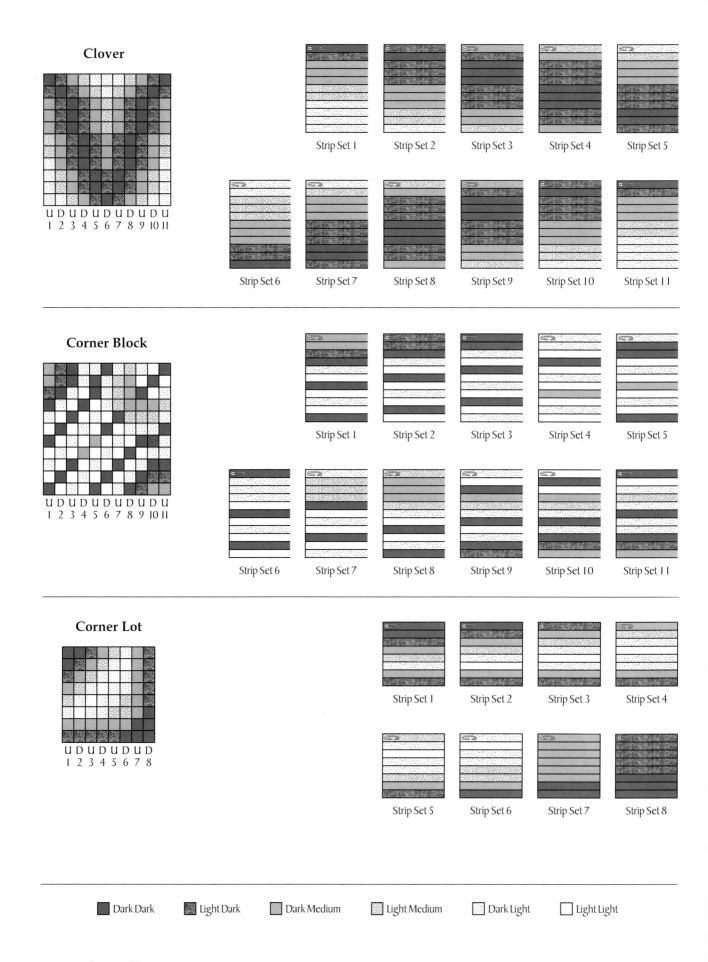

Clover

U D U D U D U D U D U
1 2 3 4 5 6 7 8 9 10 11

Strip Set 1   Strip Set 2   Strip Set 3   Strip Set 4   Strip Set 5

Strip Set 6   Strip Set 7   Strip Set 8   Strip Set 9   Strip Set 10   Strip Set 11

Corner Block

U D U D U D U D U D U
1 2 3 4 5 6 7 8 9 10 11

Strip Set 1   Strip Set 2   Strip Set 3   Strip Set 4   Strip Set 5

Strip Set 6   Strip Set 7   Strip Set 8   Strip Set 9   Strip Set 10   Strip Set 11

Corner Lot

U D U D U D U D
1 2 3 4 5 6 7 8

Strip Set 1   Strip Set 2   Strip Set 3   Strip Set 4

Strip Set 5   Strip Set 6   Strip Set 7   Strip Set 8

■ Dark Dark   ▨ Light Dark   ■ Dark Medium   ▨ Light Medium   ⬚ Dark Light   □ Light Light

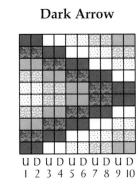

Dark Arrow

Strip Set 1   Strip Set 2   Strip Set 3   Strip Set 4   Strip Set 5

Strip Set 6   Strip Set 7   Strip Set 8   Strip Set 9   Strip Set 10

U D U D U D U D U D
1 2 3 4 5 6 7 8 9 10

Dark Line

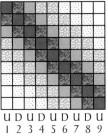

Strip Set 1   Strip Set 2   Strip Set 3   Strip Set 4

Strip Set 5   Strip Set 6   Strip Set 7   Strip Set 8   Strip Set 9

U D U D U D U D U
1 2 3 4 5 6 7 8 9

Diamonds

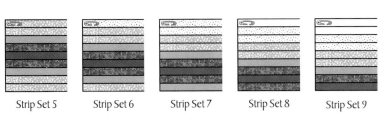

Strip Set 1   Strip Set 2   Strip Set 3   Strip Set 4   Strip Set 5

Strip Set 6   Strip Set 7   Strip Set 8   Strip Set 9   Strip Set 10   Strip Set 11

U D U D U D U D U D U
1 2 3 4 5 6 7 8 9 10 11

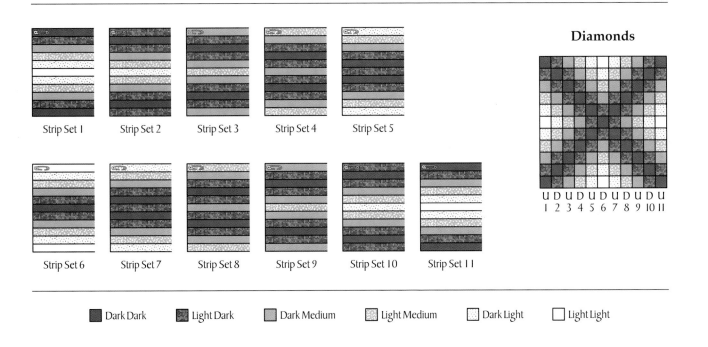

■ Dark Dark   ■ Light Dark   ■ Dark Medium   ▨ Light Medium   ▦ Dark Light   ☐ Light Light

Eight Weave

U D U D U D U D
1 2 3 4 5 6 7 8

Strip Set 1   Strip Set 2   Strip Set 3   Strip Set 4

Strip Set 5   Strip Set 6   Strip Set 7   Strip Set 8

Eleven Square One

U D U D U D U D U D U
1 2 3 4 5 6 7 8 9 10 11

Strip Set 1   Strip Set 2   Strip Set 3   Strip Set 4   Strip Set 5

Strip Set 6   Strip Set 7   Strip Set 8   Strip Set 9   Strip Set 10   Strip Set 11

ESS2

U D U D U D U D U D
1 2 3 4 5 6 7 8 9 10

Strip Set 1   Strip Set 2   Strip Set 3   Strip Set 4   Strip Set 5

Strip Set 6   Strip Set 7   Strip Set 8   Strip Set 9   Strip Set 10

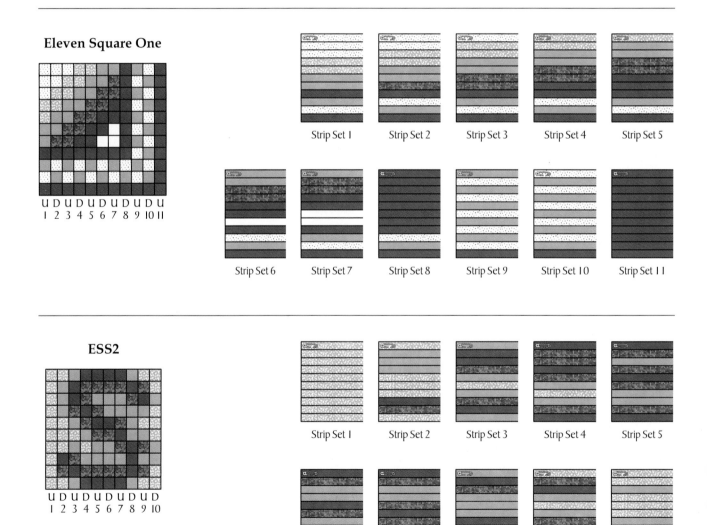

■ Dark Dark   ▨ Light Dark   ■ Dark Medium   ▨ Light Medium   ☐ Dark Light   ☐ Light Light

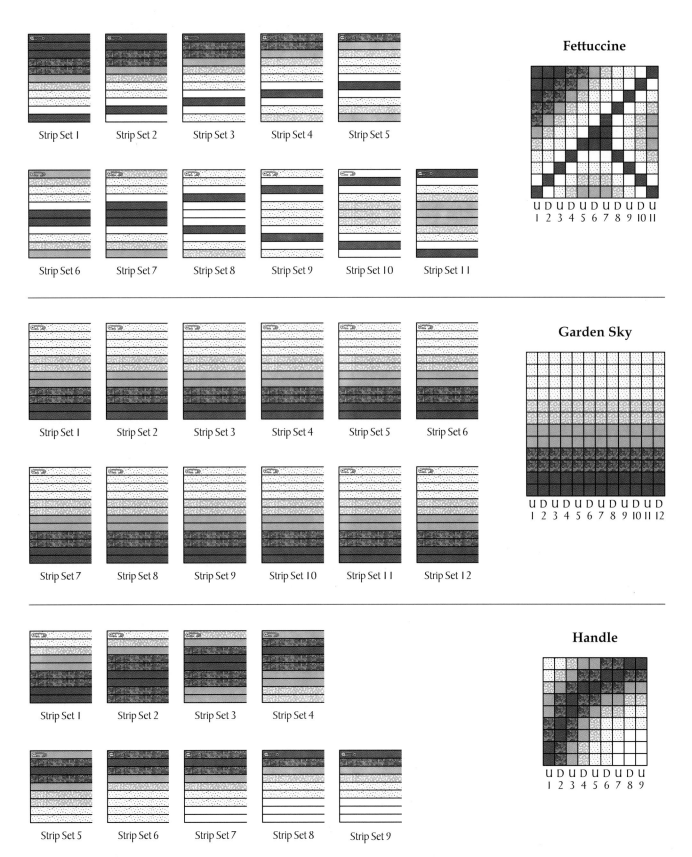

Fettuccine

u D u D u D u D u D u
1 2 3 4 5 6 7 8 9 10 11

Strip Set 1 **Strip Set 2** **Strip Set 3** **Strip Set 4** **Strip Set 5**

Strip Set 6 **Strip Set 7** **Strip Set 8** **Strip Set 9** **Strip Set 10** **Strip Set 11**

Garden Sky

u D u D u D u D u D u D
1 2 3 4 5 6 7 8 9 10 11 12

Strip Set 1 **Strip Set 2** **Strip Set 3** **Strip Set 4** **Strip Set 5** **Strip Set 6**

Strip Set 7 **Strip Set 8** **Strip Set 9** **Strip Set 10** **Strip Set 11** **Strip Set 12**

Handle

u D u D u D u D u
1 2 3 4 5 6 7 8 9

Strip Set 1 **Strip Set 2** **Strip Set 3** **Strip Set 4**

Strip Set 5 **Strip Set 6** **Strip Set 7** **Strip Set 8** **Strip Set 9**

■ Dark Dark   ▨ Light Dark   ▨ Dark Medium   ▨ Light Medium   ▨ Dark Light   □ Light Light

Hearts Two

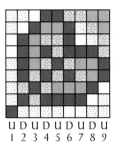

u D u D u D u D u
1 2 3 4 5 6 7 8 9

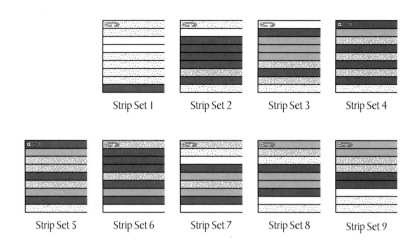

Strip Set 1   Strip Set 2   Strip Set 3   Strip Set 4

Strip Set 5   Strip Set 6   Strip Set 7   Strip Set 8   Strip Set 9

King's Crown

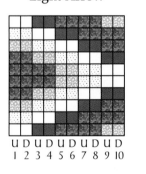

u D u D u D u
1 2 3 4 5 6 7

Strip Set 1   Strip Set 2   Strip Set 3

Strip Set 4   Strip Set 5   Strip Set 6   Strip Set 7

Light Arrow

u D u D u D u D u D
1 2 3 4 5 6 7 8 9 10

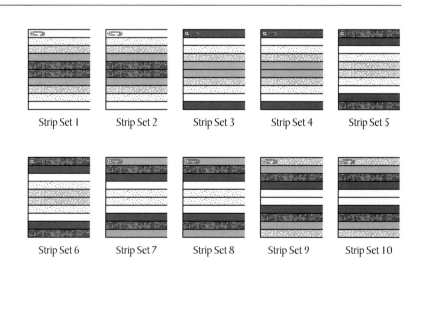

Strip Set 1   Strip Set 2   Strip Set 3   Strip Set 4   Strip Set 5

Strip Set 6   Strip Set 7   Strip Set 8   Strip Set 9   Strip Set 10

■ Dark Dark   ▩ Light Dark   ▨ Dark Medium   ▨ Light Medium   ▢ Dark Light   ☐ Light Light

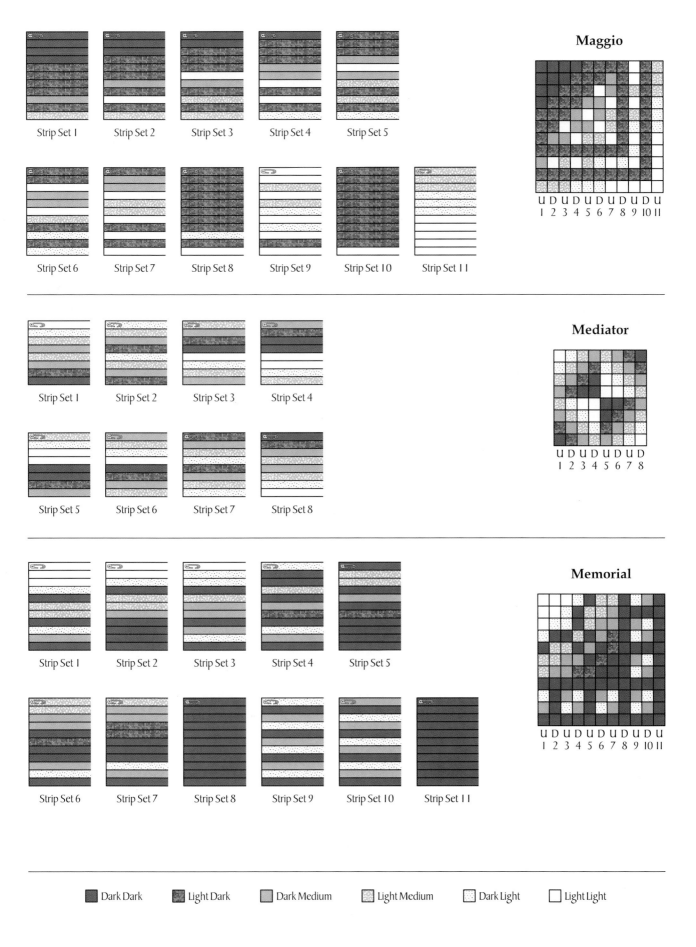

Maggio

Strip Set 1 Strip Set 2 Strip Set 3 Strip Set 4 Strip Set 5

Strip Set 6 Strip Set 7 Strip Set 8 Strip Set 9 Strip Set 10 Strip Set 11

U D U D U D U D U D U
1 2 3 4 5 6 7 8 9 10 11

Mediator

Strip Set 1 Strip Set 2 Strip Set 3 Strip Set 4

Strip Set 5 Strip Set 6 Strip Set 7 Strip Set 8

U D U D U D U D
1 2 3 4 5 6 7 8

Memorial

Strip Set 1 Strip Set 2 Strip Set 3 Strip Set 4 Strip Set 5

Strip Set 6 Strip Set 7 Strip Set 8 Strip Set 9 Strip Set 10 Strip Set 11

U D U D U D U D U D U
1 2 3 4 5 6 7 8 9 10 11

■ Dark Dark   ■ Light Dark   ■ Dark Medium   ▨ Light Medium   ▢ Dark Light   □ Light Light

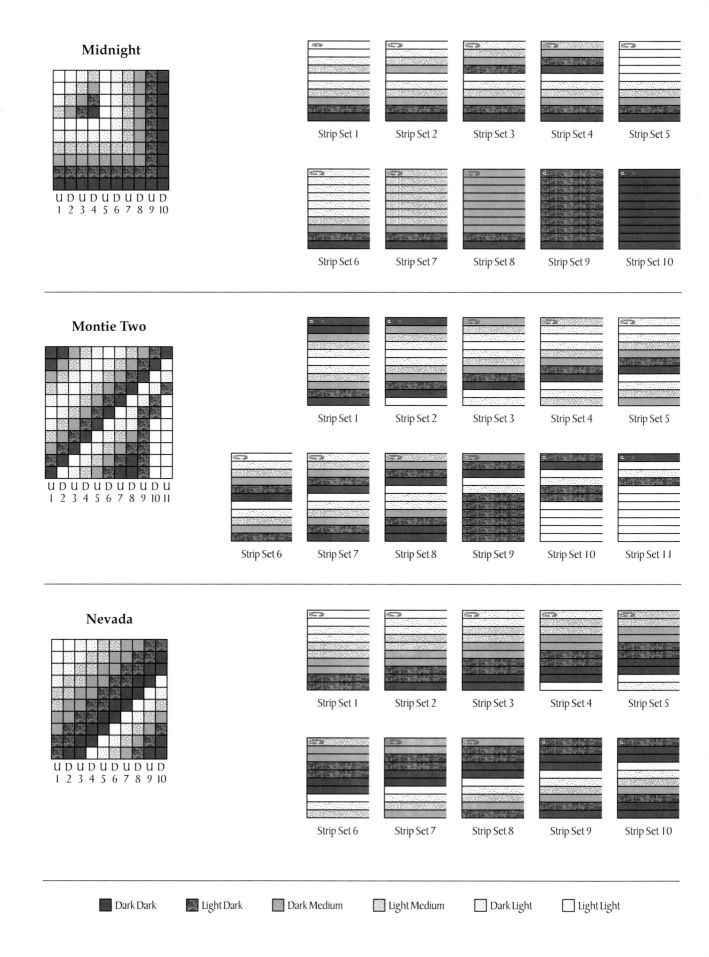

Midnight

U D U D U D U D U D
1 2 3 4 5 6 7 8 9 10

Strip Set 1   Strip Set 2   Strip Set 3   Strip Set 4   Strip Set 5

Strip Set 6   Strip Set 7   Strip Set 8   Strip Set 9   Strip Set 10

Montie Two

U D U D U D U D U D U
1 2 3 4 5 6 7 8 9 10 11

Strip Set 1   Strip Set 2   Strip Set 3   Strip Set 4   Strip Set 5

Strip Set 6   Strip Set 7   Strip Set 8   Strip Set 9   Strip Set 10   Strip Set 11

Nevada

U D U D U D U D U D
1 2 3 4 5 6 7 8 9 10

Strip Set 1   Strip Set 2   Strip Set 3   Strip Set 4   Strip Set 5

Strip Set 6   Strip Set 7   Strip Set 8   Strip Set 9   Strip Set 10

■ Dark Dark   ▨ Light Dark   ■ Dark Medium   ▨ Light Medium   ▫ Dark Light   □ Light Light

Ocho

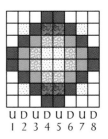

Strip Set 1   Strip Set 2   Strip Set 3   Strip Set 4

Strip Set 5   Strip Set 6   Strip Set 7   Strip Set 8

Opposition

Strip Set 1   Strip Set 2   Strip Set 3

Strip Set 4   Strip Set 5   Strip Set 6

Peaks

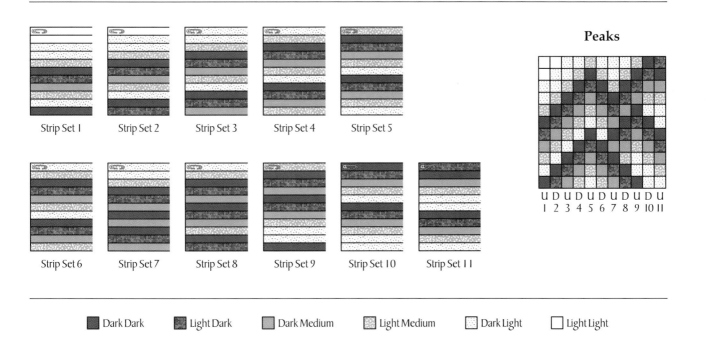

Strip Set 1   Strip Set 2   Strip Set 3   Strip Set 4   Strip Set 5

Strip Set 6   Strip Set 7   Strip Set 8   Strip Set 9   Strip Set 10   Strip Set 11

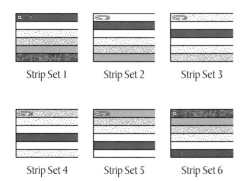

■ Dark Dark   ▨ Light Dark   ▦ Dark Medium   ▨ Light Medium   ▫ Dark Light   □ Light Light

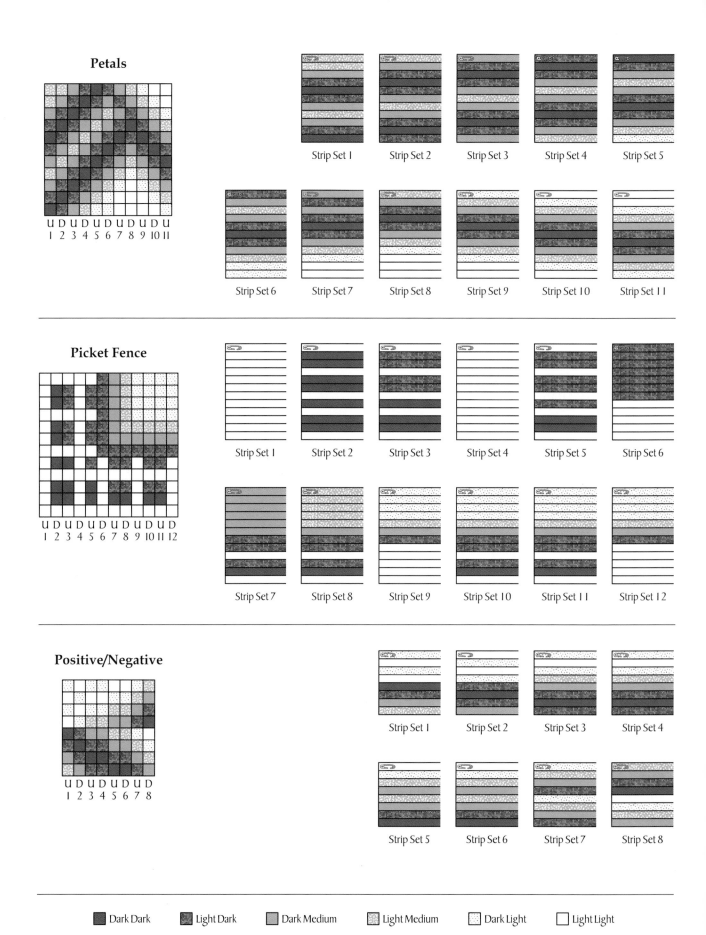

Petals

U D U D U D U D U D U
1 2 3 4 5 6 7 8 9 10 11

Strip Set 1   Strip Set 2   Strip Set 3   Strip Set 4   Strip Set 5

Strip Set 6   Strip Set 7   Strip Set 8   Strip Set 9   Strip Set 10   Strip Set 11

Picket Fence

U D U D U D U D U D U D
1 2 3 4 5 6 7 8 9 10 11 12

Strip Set 1   Strip Set 2   Strip Set 3   Strip Set 4   Strip Set 5   Strip Set 6

Strip Set 7   Strip Set 8   Strip Set 9   Strip Set 10   Strip Set 11   Strip Set 12

Positive/Negative

U D U D U D U D
1 2 3 4 5 6 7 8

Strip Set 1   Strip Set 2   Strip Set 3   Strip Set 4

Strip Set 5   Strip Set 6   Strip Set 7   Strip Set 8

■ Dark Dark   ▨ Light Dark   ■ Dark Medium   ▨ Light Medium   ⬚ Dark Light   ☐ Light Light

Queen Six

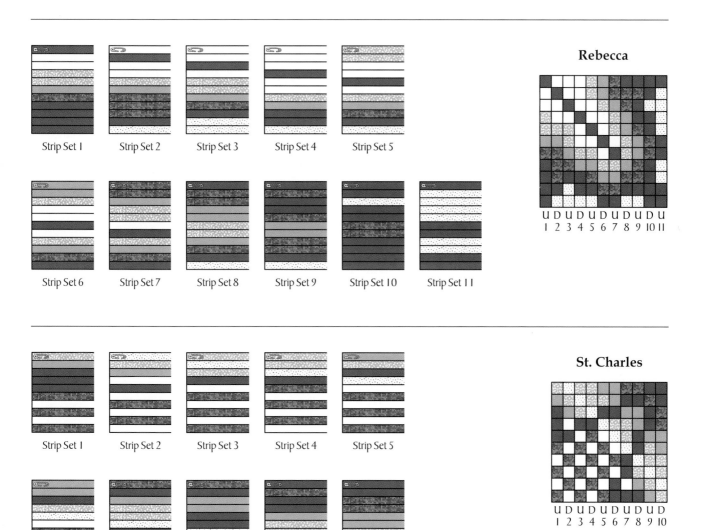

Strip Set 1 Strip Set 2 Strip Set 3

Strip Set 4 Strip Set 5 Strip Set 6

U D U D U D
1 2 3 4 5 6

Rebecca

Strip Set 1 Strip Set 2 Strip Set 3 Strip Set 4 Strip Set 5

Strip Set 6 Strip Set 7 Strip Set 8 Strip Set 9 Strip Set 10 Strip Set 11

U D U D U D U D U D U
1 2 3 4 5 6 7 8 9 10 11

St. Charles

Strip Set 1 Strip Set 2 Strip Set 3 Strip Set 4 Strip Set 5

Strip Set 6 Strip Set 7 Strip Set 8 Strip Set 9 Strip Set 10

U D U D U D U D U D
1 2 3 4 5 6 7 8 9 10

Dark Dark   Light Dark   Dark Medium   Light Medium   Dark Light   Light Light

St. Louis

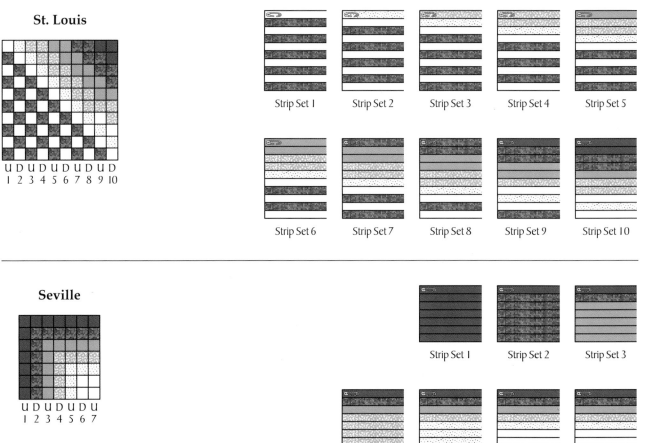

U D U D U D U D U D
1 2 3 4 5 6 7 8 9 10

Strip Set 1   Strip Set 2   Strip Set 3   Strip Set 4   Strip Set 5

Strip Set 6   Strip Set 7   Strip Set 8   Strip Set 9   Strip Set 10

Seville

U D U D U D U
1 2 3 4 5 6 7

Strip Set 1   Strip Set 2   Strip Set 3

Strip Set 4   Strip Set 5   Strip Set 6   Strip Set 7

Sioux Two

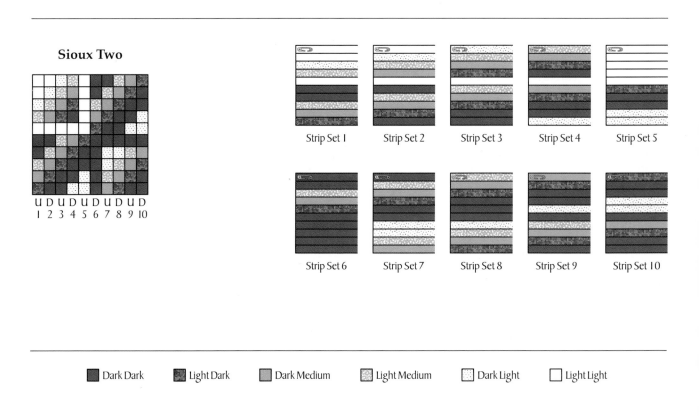

U D U D U D U D U D
1 2 3 4 5 6 7 8 9 10

Strip Set 1   Strip Set 2   Strip Set 3   Strip Set 4   Strip Set 5

Strip Set 6   Strip Set 7   Strip Set 8   Strip Set 9   Strip Set 10

■ Dark Dark   ▨ Light Dark   ▨ Dark Medium   ▨ Light Medium   ⬚ Dark Light   ☐ Light Light

Six Deep

Strip Set 1 Strip Set 2 Strip Set 3

Strip Set 4 Strip Set 5 Strip Set 6

U D U D U D
1 2 3 4 5 6

Six Square One

Strip Set 1 Strip Set 2 Strip Set 3

Strip Set 4 Strip Set 5 Strip Set 6

U D U D U D
1 2 3 4 5 6

Sonata

Strip Set 1 Strip Set 2 Strip Set 3

Strip Set 4 Strip Set 5 Strip Set 6

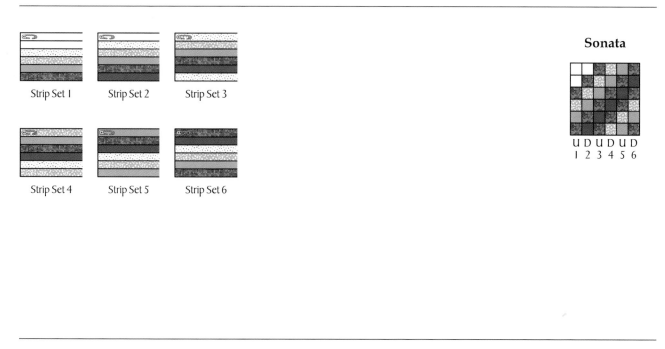

U D U D U D
1 2 3 4 5 6

■ Dark Dark ▓ Light Dark ▨ Dark Medium ▨ Light Medium ▨ Dark Light ☐ Light Light

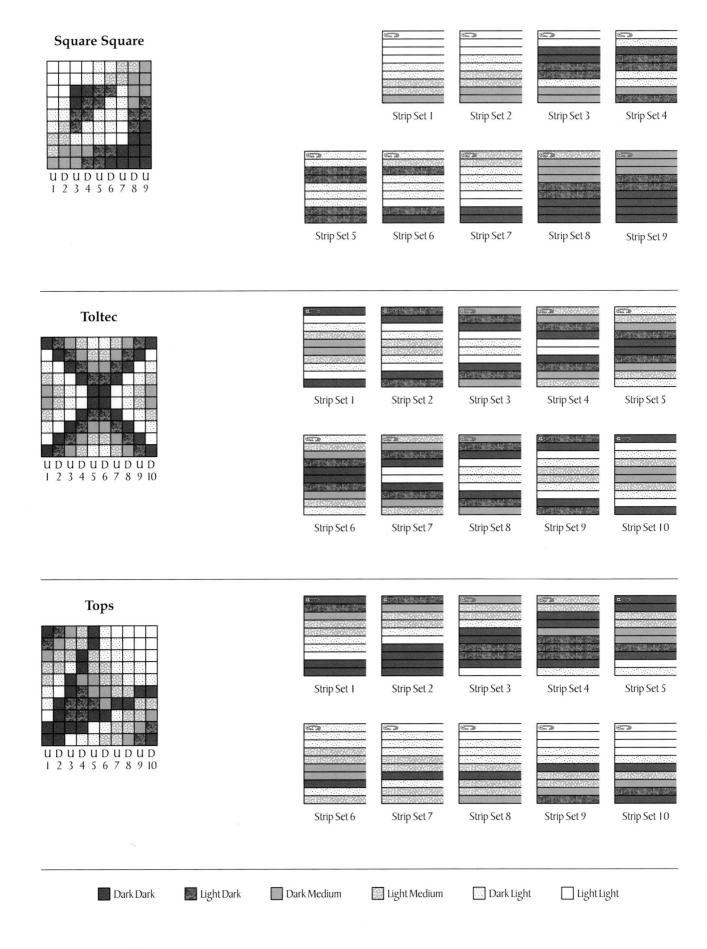

Square Square

u D u D u D u D u

1 2 3 4 5 6 7 8 9

Strip Set 1 Strip Set 2 Strip Set 3 Strip Set 4

Strip Set 5 Strip Set 6 Strip Set 7 Strip Set 8 Strip Set 9

Toltec

u D u D u D u D u D

1 2 3 4 5 6 7 8 9 10

Strip Set 1 Strip Set 2 Strip Set 3 Strip Set 4 Strip Set 5

Strip Set 6 Strip Set 7 Strip Set 8 Strip Set 9 Strip Set 10

Tops

u D u D u D u D u D

1 2 3 4 5 6 7 8 9 10

Strip Set 1 Strip Set 2 Strip Set 3 Strip Set 4 Strip Set 5

Strip Set 6 Strip Set 7 Strip Set 8 Strip Set 9 Strip Set 10

■ Dark Dark   ▨ Light Dark   ▧ Dark Medium   ▨ Light Medium   ⬚ Dark Light   ☐ Light Light

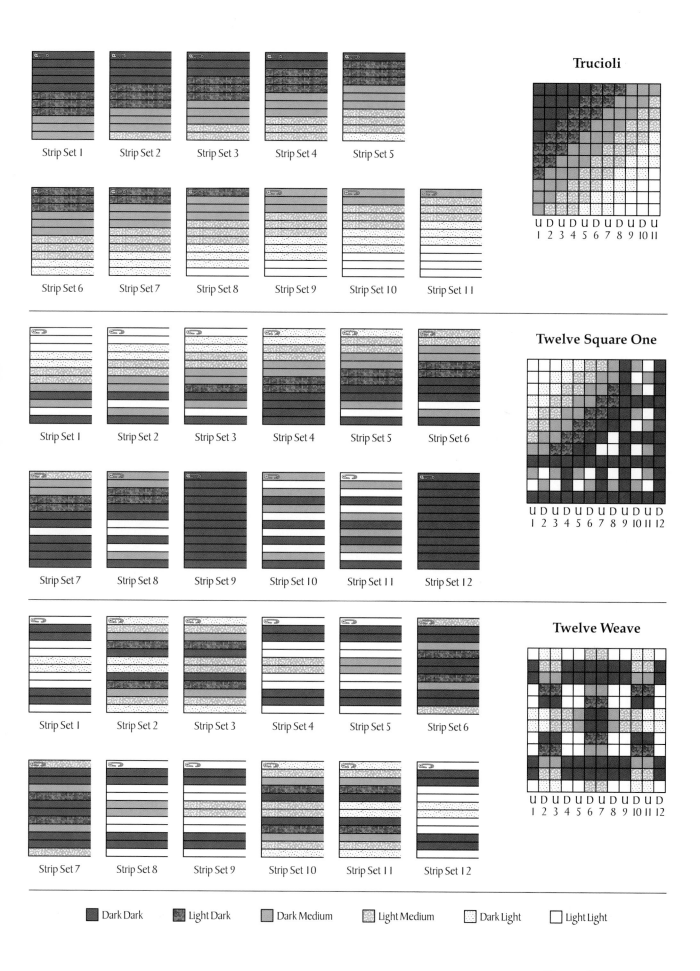

Strip Set 1
Strip Set 2
Strip Set 3
Strip Set 4
Strip Set 5

Strip Set 6
Strip Set 7
Strip Set 8
Strip Set 9
Strip Set 10
Strip Set 11

Trucioli

U D U D U D U D U D U
1 2 3 4 5 6 7 8 9 10 11

Strip Set 1
Strip Set 2
Strip Set 3
Strip Set 4
Strip Set 5
Strip Set 6

Strip Set 7
Strip Set 8
Strip Set 9
Strip Set 10
Strip Set 11
Strip Set 12

Twelve Square One

U D U D U D U D U D U D
1 2 3 4 5 6 7 8 9 10 11 12

Strip Set 1
Strip Set 2
Strip Set 3
Strip Set 4
Strip Set 5
Strip Set 6

Strip Set 7
Strip Set 8
Strip Set 9
Strip Set 10
Strip Set 11
Strip Set 12

Twelve Weave

U D U D U D U D U D U D
1 2 3 4 5 6 7 8 9 10 11 12

■ Dark Dark   ▨ Light Dark   ▩ Dark Medium   ▧ Light Medium   ░ Dark Light   □ Light Light

Unity Three

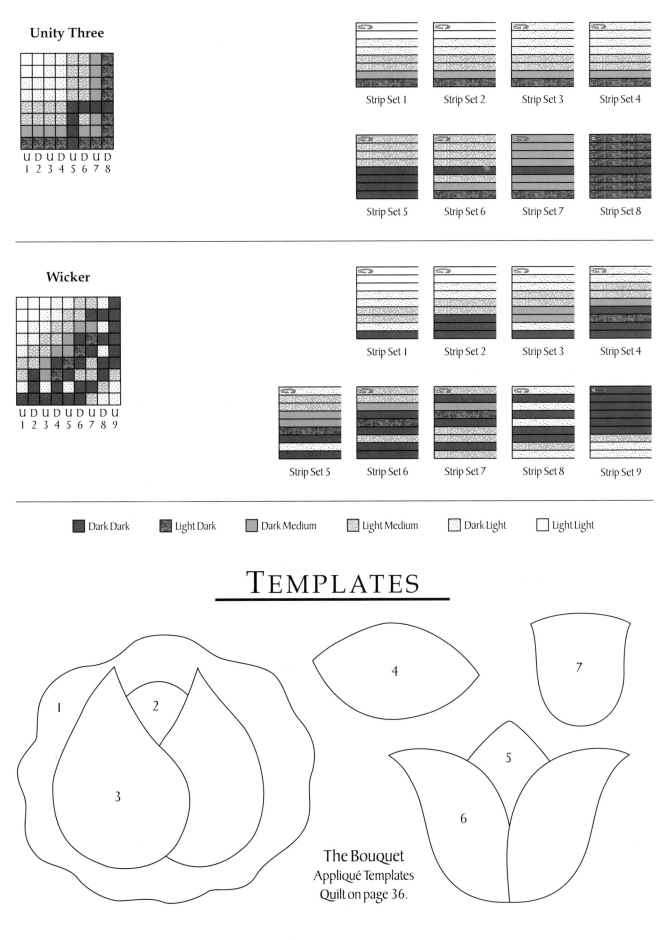

U D U D U D U D
1 2 3 4 5 6 7 8

Strip Set 1   Strip Set 2   Strip Set 3   Strip Set 4

Strip Set 5   Strip Set 6   Strip Set 7   Strip Set 8

Wicker

U D U D U D U D U
1 2 3 4 5 6 7 8 9

Strip Set 1   Strip Set 2   Strip Set 3   Strip Set 4

Strip Set 5   Strip Set 6   Strip Set 7   Strip Set 8   Strip Set 9

■ Dark Dark   ▦ Light Dark   ▨ Dark Medium   ▥ Light Medium   ⬚ Dark Light   □ Light Light

TEMPLATES

1
2
3
4
7
5
6

The Bouquet
Appliqué Templates
Quilt on page 36.

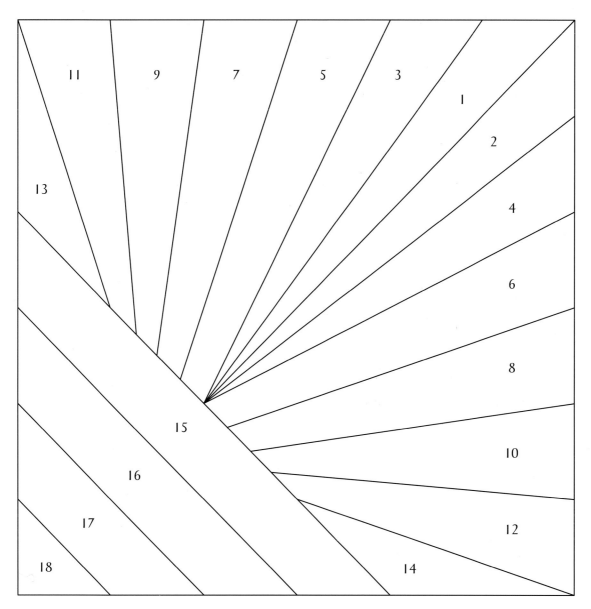

Sunrise Serenade
Foundation Piecing Block
Quilt on page 34.

Be My Valentine
Appliqué Template
Quilt on page 48.

Cut 4 ovals to make 1 flower.

Wandering Through the Fence
Appliqué Templates
Quilt on page 74.

MEET THE AUTHOR

Deanna Spingola grew up in California and bought her first sewing machine at the age of twelve. A seventh-grade sewing class motivated her to save her baby-sitting money for this major purchase. From then on, she constructed most of her own clothes. Later, she sewed for her husband and children.

What began as a worthwhile hobby later became a career. Over the years, she has taught many different sewing and design classes, including basic sewing, pattern alterations and design, and heirloom sewing. Long before the advent of the rotary cutter, she used fabric scraps from those earlier projects in her first attempt at quilting. A few years later (still pre-rotary), she had the opportunity to really learn about the traditional methods of quiltmaking.

For eight years, she worked as an independent sales representative, selling fabric, trims, and laces to fabric stores. Imagine being required to visit fabric stores every day. Currently, she enjoys traveling and teaching the methods from her popular first book, *Strip-Pieced Watercolor Magic*.

Deanna belongs to three quilt guilds: Riverwalk, Prairie Star, and Faithful Circle. She enjoys cooking, creative writing, reading, sewing, and genealogical research. She has four grown children. She and her husband, Bob, live in a Chicago suburb. Between them, they have eight wonderful grandchildren.